MY UNCLE FULTON SHEEN

MY UNCLE FULTON SHEEN

By Joan Sheen Cunningham

With Janel Rodriguez

IGNATIUS PRESS   SAN FRANCISCO

Portrait of Bishop Fulton J. Sheen, 1957
© Yousuf Karsh

Cover design by Riz Boncan Marsella

© 2020 by Ignatius Press, San Francisco
All rights reserved
ISBN 978-1-58617-820-8 (PB)
ISBN 978-1-64229-110-0 (eBook)
Library of Congress Control Number 2015930772
Printed in the United States of America ∞

CONTENTS

NOTE FROM THE COAUTHOR

Much of this book consists of the memories of Joan Sheen Cunningham from when she was a child and young adult, and therefore of when she didn't have a full understanding of what her uncle was achieving in the outside world and why he was famous. Therefore, between each chapter I have supplied some biographical and historical information to give the reader a fuller picture of just who Fulton Sheen was, why he may shortly be canonized a saint in the Catholic Church, and why Joan is so blessed to be able to call him her uncle.

Janel Rodriguez

FOREWORD

Joan Sheen Cunningham's book, *My Uncle Fulton Sheen*, should be essential reading for anyone interested in the life and heroic Christian witness of Sheen. When I was a Holy Cross novice way back in 1966, I believe that his *Life of Christ* was the very first of his many wonderful books that I read. Like so many others growing up in the 1950s, however, I was first introduced to Bishop Sheen while watching with my family his *Life Is Worth Living* TV series. I'm not sure how much I actually understood, but like many other Catholic kids at the time, I enjoyed his opening jokes; his dramatic style; the JMJ (Jesus, Mary, and Joseph) that he always scrolled at the top of his blackboard, just as we did on our school tests and papers; and I hoped to catch sight of his angel whom he claimed did his erasing.

In later years as a seminarian, then as a priest and bishop, and especially in these last eighteen years that I have had the privilege to serve as the petitioner of his cause for canonization and the head of the Fulton Sheen Foundation, I have been enormously blessed to read much more of his writing, listen to many of his tapes, and be well instructed by viewing copies of his television presentations.

He certainly should be numbered among the great minds of his generation, but I also believe that his truly extraordinary gift was to communicate profound truths in a way that was accessible to ordinary people. His clear teaching continues to be relevant and even prescient for today, but my own prejudice is that he can still be watched

at the very top of his form as a communicator in his orig-
inal black-and-white TV series.

Reading Joan's fascinating account of her beloved
uncle's story gives a richly human context to the inspiring
life of this good, gifted, and holy man. Please pray with
me that Blessed Fulton Sheen may, in the language of our
tradition, soon *be raised to the altars* of the Church.

Sincerely yours in Christ,
✠ Most Reverend Daniel R. Jenky, C.S.C.
Bishop of Peoria

PREFACE

Here are my memories of my uncle Fulton Sheen. I wish to thank Janel Rodriguez for patiently listening to my stories and for piecing it all together in a book that others can read.

Looking back on it all, I realize what was most important about the time I spent with Fulton Sheen. It was not the interesting places I visited or the fascinating people I met, but the lessons my uncle taught me about living. He taught me not by his preaching but by his example. He was always understanding, forgiving, and generous with others—and not just with material things. He encouraged me to act in the same way. He wanted me to give of myself (as he gave of himself in imitation of Christ), and he often reminded me that the simple gifts of a visit, a smile, and a kind word "can do wonders". While I may not have always succeeded in living out all that he taught me, I still remember the lessons.

Another thing he taught me was to say, "God is good," in every circumstance. I can't help but believe that God is good—especially when I think of the blessing that my uncle was in my life.

I hope that in his goodness God wills that my uncle be named a saint in the Catholic Church. Please pray with me for the canonization of Archbishop Fulton J. Sheen:

> Heavenly Father, source of all holiness, you raise up within the Church in every age men and women who serve with heroic love and dedication. You have blessed

your Church through the life and ministry of your faithful servant, Archbishop Fulton J. Sheen. He has written and spoken well of your Divine Son, Jesus Christ, and was a true instrument of the Holy Spirit in touching the hearts of countless people. If it be according to your will, for the honor and glory of the most Holy Trinity and for the salvation of souls, we ask you to move the Church to proclaim him a saint. We make this prayer through Jesus Christ Our Lord. Amen. (The Archbishop Fulton John Sheen Foundation, Peoria, IL)

God love you.

Joan Sheen Cunningham

INTRODUCTION

The determining mold of my early life was the decision of my parents that each of their children should be well educated.

—Fulton J. Sheen, *Treasure in Clay*

I was ten years old when my father took me aside—away from my brothers and sister—to ask me the question that would change the course of my life. But he first went about it slowly, beginning with a little talk about my uncle Fulton Sheen.

He wanted me to know just how special he thought my uncle was. But my father didn't have to convince me. I already believed my uncle was special—and not just because when he visited us he gave us children candy and gifts.

He was a priest. A man of such dignity and holiness that even his own brother—my father—expressed a deep respect for him. His respect ran so deep, in fact, that we children were instructed never to call him "uncle" but "Father" (and later by his other religious titles of "Monsignor" and "Bishop"). Nevertheless, I was still perfectly comfortable around my uncle because I also knew him to be a fun—and funny—person. He had a ready sense of humor and the most infectious belly laugh.

I had gotten to know that side of him well because my family and I had recently spent some weeks with him enjoying the summer holidays together, and during the trip my uncle and I really hit it off. We just clicked—perhaps because we shared similar personality traits. For instance, like him, I enjoyed traveling, meeting people, and learning new things. We seemed to understand each other.

The connection had not gone unnoticed by my father and my uncle, and they came up with a bold and brilliant idea. My father took me aside and explained that even though my uncle enjoyed children and family life, as a priest, he could never have children or a family of his own. He could, however, offer me the wonderful opportunity of a grand Catholic education in New York City.

If I agreed to attend a school there, he said, even though I would be far away from the rest of my family (who would remain in Illinois), I would be able to spend the weekends with my uncle, accompanying him to church, events, and dinners, and discovering the sights and sounds of the city with him. In that way, we both would be able to enjoy the bonds of family life. "You could be like a daughter to him," my father said.

My uncle joined us to discuss the plan further. The school was run by the Society of the Holy Child Jesus, an international order of sisters founded in England in 1846. He had tremendous respect for them and the sort of education they could provide me. During the week, he explained, instead of boarding at the school, I would stay with longtime friends of his who had a girl my age. During holidays, vacations, and summers I would be home.

Finally, he asked, "Do you have any questions or hesitancy about this idea?"

"Oh no," I said. I didn't. I simply had no qualms whatsoever.

"So," my father said, winking at me encouragingly, "how does it all sound to you?"

I thought it sounded like an adventure.

THE FAMILY SHEEN

*Children ... become as beads in the great rosary of love,
chaining father and mother together in the sweetest slavery
of all, which is the love of a family and the happiness of
a home.*

—Fulton J. Sheen, *Life Is Worth Living*

There were eight of us children all together, a typical Irish
Catholic family at the time. My uncle helped to support
the education of all of his nieces and nephews, but due to
timing and favorable circumstances, I was the only one
who enjoyed the unique opportunity of a Catholic education in New York City during its golden age. And it was
all thanks to the kind and generous efforts of a saint—who
also happened to be my uncle.

But before all that happened, I was just a girl from La
Grange, a western suburb of Chicago. Both my parents
were from Peoria, Illinois, where I was born on June 27,
1927. I was the third child and the first girl. We were
(in order): Joseph Jr., John, Joan (me), Bob, Sue, Fulton,
Tommy, and Karen. My uncle Fulton Sheen had already
been a priest for eight years by the time I was born, and
he baptized me.

Uncle Fulton was the oldest of four sons. Being born
second, my father was the brother closest to him. My

uncle's real first name, by the way, was Peter. That's right: he was baptized Peter John Sheen. Here is the story he would tell to explain how he came to be known by his mother's maiden name: "This is how I got the name Fulton. I was baptized Peter. I cried so much that I was a constant burden to my mother and my father. To get a little relief, they used to take me to my grandparents, whose [last] name was Fulton. I got to be known as 'Fulton's baby'. Later on the 'baby' and then the apostrophe were dropped, and I became just plain Fulton."

My Parents

Both "Fulton" and "Sheen" were family names. So much so, in fact, that my father once worked for the family law firm, Fulton, Fulton & Sheen. Yes, my father, Joseph Sheen, was a lawyer. He had a general practice, where he did a lot of insurance work, wills, and that sort of thing. He did some trial work, too, when he was younger, but he did less and less of that as he got older.

My mother, Anne, was a homemaker. With eight children she had her work cut out for her, but she had a calm personality and was not easily ruffled. She had worked as a secretary before she married my father, and whenever my father's secretary took a vacation, my mother would slip into her chair while she was away. I learned from my mother's example, and later in life I helped my husband (who was also a lawyer) with paperwork and other things whenever I was needed. My mother was quite capable and smart—a great help to my father. The two of them were very close. True partners in life.

My childhood was full and happy. It was a simpler time. We enjoyed a lot of family fun together, playing games such as cards and checkers. (Though I must say, it seemed as though my mother always won. She was the champion of the family. And later in life when she became a bridge player, she was once again the champion.)

When our father came home from work, we always sat down to supper together as a family. He would tell us how his day went and explain some of the cases he was working on. In the course of a story he would often ask, "What would you do in this situation?" He wanted us to learn how to think and to solve problems. We had many interesting conversations around the dinner table this way.

When I was only in elementary school, I participated in these conversations along with my older brothers, and some of them were quite involved. Seeing my interest and abilities, my father said I should consider pursuing a career in law. He was a man ahead of his time to be encouraging his daughter to follow in his footsteps. This sort of thing was practically unheard of in the 1930s. Had it been another time, perhaps I would have done it. As it was, once I met my future husband I gave little thought to studying law.

My father's profession required him to deal with very serious matters, but he had a great sense of humor (a trait he shared with my uncle). We had a lot of laughs growing up, and some of them were at his expense. For instance, once when he tried to make fudge and it wouldn't harden, he left it out in the snow. Needless to say, the experiment didn't work.

Cooking was more my mother's talent—as was music. She loved to play the piano and was quite good at it. To entertain ourselves, the family would often gather around the piano and sing together. A family of our size made for a pretty decent-sized choir.

We were sure to all be very quiet, however, whenever my uncle was on the radio. At that time, he was on a program called *The Catholic Hour*. (Actually, he was on it for more than twenty years.) While not the only speaker on the hour-long program (his weekly contribution usually lasted about twenty minutes), he quickly "stole" the show with his learned manner, informed talks, and helpful answers to listeners' questions. *The Catholic Hour* had millions of regular listeners, and it made my uncle famous.

Even though the famous Fulton Sheen was a close relative, familiarity with him did not diminish my parents' respect for him. My parents saw him as a gifted teacher, and my father explained to us children that his lessons had a lot to teach us, too, that we should listen to him as attentively as his other listeners across the United States (and even the world, thanks to shortwave radios).

Practicing Lawyer, Practicing Catholic

My father had a reputation as a good lawyer in the Chicago area, and his Catholic faith was one of the reasons for this. In those days, people treated their lawyers almost like doctors. Sometimes my father would be "sent for" to make a "house call". If this happened at night, we sometimes got in the car with him and stayed there while he paid his visit.

As a family we were very proud of our Irish heritage, but we were also brought up to be respectful of people with different backgrounds. I guess my father had been raised that way, too. My uncle's work for the missions and his travels all over the world on behalf of the Society for the Propagation of the Faith were just about his favorite things to do. He loved people of all kinds and helping them as much as they could, and so did my father.

My father had a number of Chinese clients, and every Chinese New Year, they invited him to bring his family to Chicago's Chinatown in order to join them in their celebrations. We would get dressed up and bring presents to exchange with people we often couldn't understand. They didn't understand us either, so it was mutual. No one seemed to mind, and we had a great time together anyway. Plus, the food was delicious!

I think this exposure to different cultures at a young age was good for me and my siblings. It broadened our view of the world and helped us to appreciate the diversity in the human family. Besides, respecting every person and treating him the same way one would like to be treated is the Christian way to live.

We were well aware of the reality of prejudice based on race and religion. For one thing, we Catholics were living in a mostly Protestant town. Although we were tolerated, Jewish and black families were not allowed to buy homes there. We knew two African American families who literally lived on the other side of the tracks and worked as domestics. A group of townspeople got together and paid for their children's tuition so that they could attend the Catholic school. I have a hunch that my father played a role in this act of charity, for he valued all people as equals. My mother did, too. She didn't bat an eye when my brothers brought a black classmate home from school to have lunch with them.

My uncle championed the cause of equal treatment for all in the 1950s, before the civil rights movement was in full swing. On an episode of his television show, *Life Is Worth Living*, he said,

> If there is anything that makes me feel sad at heart, it is to see a cartoon or a drawing or a picture, for example, of a Chinese child, a Japanese child, an American Child, and

underneath it the caption reads, "Be tolerant." A person is the most precious thing in the universe. A person is made in the image and likeness of God: every person bears within himself the Divine resemblance. The state exists for the person, and not the person for the state. No Irishman is to be tolerated! No Jew is to be tolerated! No American is to be tolerated! No German is to be tolerated! As persons, they are all to be loved.

Life on the Farm

Having only boys, my paternal grandmother, Delia, was thrilled to gain a "daughter" when my mother married one of her sons, and they became very close. She was even more thrilled when I, the first granddaughter, was born, and she was further delighted when my sisters came along. Finally, there were some girls in the family, and she intended to enjoy them. When school was out, my grandmother frequently invited us to the farm where my father and his brothers spent their childhoods.

It is a well-known fact that my uncle Fulton was not made for farm life. He may have been born into it, but he never took to it and it never took to him. Or as he wrote in his autobiography, *Treasure in Clay*, "My brothers rather enjoyed farm work; I suffered it.... I ... argued with my father every day that farming was not a good life and that you could make a fortune on it only if you struck oil." He much preferred reading books to wringing chickens' necks! He couldn't grow up and move away fast enough.

But we, his nieces and nephews, loved the farm. The rustic life was so different from our suburban existence. No electricity, no indoor plumbing (which means using an outhouse)—it was all an adventure to us. We could pretend to be pioneers. We seemed to have inherited some of the Sheen farming gene.

Our father certainly had. He enjoyed planting things and teaching us all he could about the farm. Actually, it was a cluster of small, separate farms, which was left to him and his three brothers when their father died. My uncle Fulton did not want his portion of the land (what would he do with a farm?), so his brothers bought him out. Fulton used the money to buy himself a house in Washington, D.C., which proved to be a savvy decision as he would live there for twenty years.

My other uncles entrusted the management of their farms to my father, who fulfilled that responsibility until he died. He set up a number of his cousins as tenant farmers who lived there and tended the land. Everyone benefited from the arrangement.

I truly enjoyed working on the farm. I thought that helping my mother to detassel ears of corn was great fun. Detasseling is removing the pollen-producing tops, or tassels, from the young corn plants. This is done to control which plants pollinate, in order to raise hybrids for seed.

On Saturday evenings, we would take a break from our labors to go to the movies. A big screen would be set up in a field, and we would bring chairs and snacks and enjoy an open-air theatre experience. We thought it was just grand. Sometimes the very next week we would be home in the suburbs again and end up watching a movie in an air-conditioned theatre. It was quite a contrast.

Growing up Catholic

My siblings and I attended grammar school at Saint Francis Xavier in La Grange. Too bad there weren't enough Catholics in town to fill the parish's huge, beautiful church.

My parents were very close friends with a non-Catholic couple who were having difficulties with their son, Don, who was very spoiled, and they decided to send him to our Catholic school for some discipline. Plus, his friends (my brothers) could keep an eye on him there. Well, they did. One day they came home from school and told my mother, "You don't have to worry about Don anymore. He'll go to Heaven."

In her usual calm manner my mother asked, "Why do you say he will go to Heaven?"

"Because we baptized him!" they announced.

While playing outside, they explained, they taught Don all about baptism. Then they baptized him with the closest water that was available: rainwater from the gutter. For years we laughed about their "baptizing" Don. Funnier still is the fact that later in life Don actually became a Catholic! Apparently my brothers inherited some of their uncle Fulton's ability to convert hearts and bring people to the Church.

At Saint Francis all the students were required to attend Mass before school started. One cold, snowy morning in Lent, our father decided to drive us to school in order to spare us the inconvenience of walking in the snow. Since he attended an earlier morning Mass at a different church, he took me, my brothers, and their friend Larry along with him there. Afterward he dropped us off at school and drove to his office.

When we entered Saint Francis Xavier Church, the Mass wasn't finished yet. In fact, it was time for Communion. We stood awkwardly at the back of the church, unsure of what to do next. We had been taught that it was wrong to receive Communion more than once in a single day, so we didn't want to make that mistake. On the other hand, it also somehow felt "wrong" not to get in the Communion line—almost as if we were rejecting Christ.

As we all privately struggled with the dilemma of our confusing situation, a nun spotted us and made things worse. She was named (coincidentally enough) Sister Eucharistic, and she was a little spitfire. After she caught sight of us, she immediately charged up the aisle. "Get up to that altar!" she ordered. She practically pushed us all the way to the Communion rail. None of us dared to resist her.

When the priest came along and held up the Host to my oldest brother, the rest of us watched him intently. My brother meekly accepted the Host on his tongue, and one by one, the rest of us followed suit. But we were all in a panic. We were disobeying Church teaching! As soon as we could, we all ran out the side door and to the home of a neighbor we all knew well and said, "You've got to get a hold of our mother because we all just committed a terrible sin!"

She rang her up, and soon our mother was with us, hearing our story as it all tumbled out. But my mother wasn't sure what to do either. "You need to tell the priest," she said. So the troop of us went to the priest to confess our transgression.

He was very understanding. He hadn't realized we had already received Communion and assured us we weren't going to be excommunicated. What a relief!

Uncle Fulton and I

I'm sure my uncle Fulton would have told us the same thing had we asked him for his priestly advice. And years later he became my go-to priest whenever I had a question about the faith or its practices. I became as comfortable around him as my own father. In fact, I would come to see him as my "second father". But that came later.

When I was very young, Uncle Fulton visited us, of course, but not too often because he lived in Washington, D.C. On one of his more memorable visits, he brought me a little dog. He loved dogs—but only big loping ones that knocked into things and drooled. He didn't much like small dogs. He especially didn't like them when they were particularly yappy, and this little dog was. I suppose that someone must have given this dog to Uncle Fulton and that he was eager to part with it.

It may have been small enough to be considered a lap-dog, but this dog didn't care much for laps. He cared more for seat cushions—or, to be more precise, the seat cushion on my father's chair. After a while, whenever my father came home from a long day of work and wanted to sit down, the dog tried to push him out of his chair. Not one of us was very happy with him.

I don't know what became of that dog. It just disappeared one day. My parents must have given it away, because if it had died, we would have had a "funeral" for it. Whenever one of our pets died, we would process about with a kind of hurdy-gurdy (an instrument that plays music as its handle is turned) and then bury the little creature in the backyard. If the animal was small enough, it was laid to rest in a "coffin" made from a cigar box. Over time we had quite a number of animals buried in our little graveyard, including Bozo the chicken.

Bozo had been a gift from the farm. Our grandparents had given us a bunch of chicks one Easter, and I named mine Bozo. For some reason, all the other chicks died, making Bozo the sole survivor and my special pet. She grew rather large, and I became very attached to her. Seeing this, my father made her a collar so that I could take her for walks like a dog! "Joan," he would call when friends came over, "show them your pet!" Of course everyone laughed when they saw a chicken with a collar around its neck.

One day, while out for a walk with Bozo, a dog attacked the chicken and killed it. That was a very, very sad day in our lives. We buried Bozo in the backyard and marked her little grave with a cross made of sticks.

When I was about eight years old, my grandparents took me along on a visit to Uncle Fulton in Washington, D.C. He showed us the famous landmarks, and as he was very knowledgeable about history, he naturally made a great tour guide. He also gave us a tour of the Catholic University of America, where he worked as a philosophy professor for twenty years.

I did not find him bookish as some might imagine a philosophy professor. He was a very well-rounded person. On this trip, for example, I learned of his passion for playing tennis, which was his favorite form of exercise. When *Life* magazine published a feature story about my uncle Fulton in the 1950s, it included a photo of him in his tennis clothes.

The following year my parents decided to visit my uncle in Washington. When they said I could come along, I was overjoyed. I didn't mind at all seeing the same sights as before.

The summer I was ten, before I began my schooling in New York and before anyone had even thought of the idea, Uncle Fulton invited my family to New Jersey. He would be giving a series of retreat talks at the Church of Saint Ann, and he would be staying at a large summer home beside a lake owned by a family he knew.

"You've got to come," he said. "There's a swimming pool and all sorts of activities like sports and dancing lessons for young people."

So we went. And did I have fun.

This trip was not unusual. Whenever my uncle was going to preach or to give a retreat at a location he thought the rest of us might enjoy, he invited us to join him. Because we were a large family, all of us couldn't always go, but my brothers and I (the three eldest children) often could. We stayed at a Catholic Action summer camp in upstate New York while our uncle was a speaker there, and once we went with him to Canada.

My uncle genuinely liked children. In an episode of his *Life Is Worth Living* television program, he famously said, "Children rescue love from boredom." He was always very good-natured and patient with us. Whenever he corrected me, he did so in a gentle manner, and I wouldn't feel badly about having made a mistake. I don't remember him ever getting upset with me.

One time when we were traveling, he asked me to help him pack his robes. I valiantly tried to fold one of his heavy capes, but I couldn't manage it. When he caught sight of me struggling, he said, "Oh, no, no, no! Just roll them up in a ball and stick them in the suitcase. They always turn out fine!"

Over the course of my travels with Uncle Fulton, we forged a wonderful rapport. So it did not seem unnatural at all, to me or the rest of my family, when he offered to enroll me in a school in New York. To me, it sounded like another grand experience in the making—and it surely was that and more.

The Education of Fulton J. Sheen

Fulton Sheen's desire that his niece receive the best education that she could can be traced to his parents' aspirations for their children. Newton and Delia Sheen had not moved beyond lower and middle school, respectively, and early in their marriage they began raising wheat and corn to make ends meet. While they took pride in their work (and their strong work ethic was another trait their son Fulton inherited), life was a struggle. They not only hoped for more for their sons, but firmly believed that for them education would be the path to future success.

In fact, the Sheens moved to Peoria in order to enroll both Fulton and Joseph (Joan's father) in Catholic school at Saint Mary's. Education was a necessity in Fulton's case, for it became painfully obvious early on that Fulton had no knack for farm life—and no love for it either. Although he obediently performed his chores daily—plowing fields, milking cows, feeding pigs, mucking stalls, tending to injured animals, harvesting crops, and so on—he complained often that it was no way to make a living.

One of his most hated chores was killing chickens for meals. He once jokingly estimated that he had wrung the necks of 22,413 chickens. These experiences put him off poultry, and once he was an adult and on his own, he refused to eat chicken ever again. If it was served to him in someone's home, he would push it around his plate so that it would appear as though he had eaten some of it.

The Young Scholar

As poor as he was at farming, he was good at academics. He was a star pupil who shone at a young age and in many subjects: spelling, arithmetic, history, and religion. He seemed to have a nearly photographic memory; for example, he could recall entire trigonometry problems from his textbook. His talent for public speaking revealed itself early, too, and resulted in his being on the school debate team. Almost predictably, he was the valedictorian at his high school, Spalding Institute.

Many of Fulton's best childhood memories centered on the academic success he achieved through his Catholic education. One can see why he wanted such an education for his nieces and nephews and was so confident that Joan would benefit intellectually, emotionally, and spiritually from attending a top-flight Catholic school in New York.

Between his parents and school, Fulton grew up immersed in the faith. His parents (particularly his mother, Delia) were devout Catholics who led their family in praying the Rosary every night. Fulton served in the Cathedral of Saint Mary of the Immaculate Conception as an altar boy, and the family had priests from the cathedral over for dinner as often as once a week. So growing up, Fulton had many opportunities to meet and observe well-educated priests, which obviously both influenced and impressed him a great deal.

Vocation

A man does not become a priest by choice, the way he might choose a career. A vocation to the priesthood is a prompting from God, which a man receives as an inner knowing that Christ is asking him to follow in his foot-steps. Fulton heard the call so early in life that later he would say he could not remember a time when he did not know that he wanted to be a priest. It was an aspiration he kept to himself for years, however. He secretly prayed for the vocation after receiving his First Communion at the age of twelve. He did not reveal his desire until he was about to enter Saint Viator College, in Bourbonnais, Illinois, which had a seminary. His parents then said that they had long prayed that he would become a priest—if it was his vocation. Their only advice? "Be a good one."

While at Saint Viator, Fulton found good priests to emulate. In particular, Father Gerald Bergan, who taught philosophy, became "one of the greatest inspirations" of his life. Like him, Fulton became both a priest and a pro-fessor of philosophy.

Fulton completed his studies for the priesthood at Saint Paul Seminary in Minnesota. He was ordained a priest on Saturday, September 20, 1919, back home in Peoria. Immediately afterward, he went to the Catholic Univer-sity of America in Washington, D.C., where he obtained bachelor's degrees in theology and canon law. Next, he went to the Catholic University of Leuven, Belgium, for doctoral studies in philosophy.

At Leuven (or Louvain, as the French—and Fulton—called it), he rejoiced in the comprehensiveness of their courses, which covered all the milestones of philosophy from ancient Greece to the Middle Ages to the modern era. He said that he read "every single line that St. Thomas [Aquinas] wrote at least once." He thrived in the scholarly atmosphere, absorbing all that he could, and he graduated with the "very highest distinction" in 1923.

Next, Sheen went to Rome, where he earned a sacred theology doctorate at the Pontificium Collegium

Internationale Angelicum, the future Pontifical University of Saint Thomas Aquinas, known simply as the Angelicum. He then spent a year as the assistant to the pastor of Saint Patrick's Catholic Church in Soho Square, London, while teaching theology at Saint Edmund's College, a private high school for boys, in Ware. There he met Father Ronald Knox, who had left the Anglican priesthood to become a Catholic. Like Sheen, he went on to become a famous author and radio personality.

Although both Oxford and Columbia offered Sheen teaching positions, in 1925 his bishop assigned him to be the assistant pastor of Saint Patrick's Church in Peoria. Although Sheen would have preferred the prestigious academic posts, he believed that by following his bishop's orders he was doing the will of God. He poured his knowledge and talent for teaching into his sermons, which got him noticed by both the local press (which criticized the bishop for "wasting" the gifted young curate) and the congregation (which grew from four to ninety people). What none of them knew was that the bishop Edmund Dunne had been testing Sheen's obedience.

Sheen passed the test, and after nine months, Bishop Dunne returned him to the Catholic University of America to become a professor. He first joined the faculty of the School of Theology, but because he did not have a doctorate in that subject, he was transferred to the School of Philosophy, where he would teach for more than two decades.

The Professor

Fulton would prepare for hours before any lecture by praying, researching, and even practicing his arguments in another language—such as Latin or French—to make sure that he knew his stuff. He never sat when he lectured because he believed that "fires cannot be started seated." And he wanted to inflame his listeners with an enthusiastic understanding of the faith.

He was known to challenge his students. Rather than simply telling them what is true and what is false, he would ask them questions and invite them to explain what they thought was true. If he disagreed with their stated positions, he would skillfully dismantle their arguments without ever insulting or patronizing them.

On a visit to a state university, he spoke to thousands of students about the virtue of chastity. He deftly, yet respectfully, chipped away at the arguments in favor of sexual license, and by the end, the students erupted into applause in recognition of the truth of his words and the consideration with which he spoke them.

"The more divine the talk and the more the talk is related to the Crucifixion of Our Lord, the more it involves the unknown element of self-sacrifice to our modern pagans, the more responsive they are," he once observed. "I beg Him every day to keep me strong physically and alert mentally in order to preach the Gospel and proclaim His Cross and Resurrection."

The Paulist Fathers of New York heard of his abilities and in 1928 invited him to give a series of talks that would be broadcast over the local radio station. The talks went so well that the series, which was only supposed to run for some weeks, was extended by some years.

Next, he was invited to become a featured speaker on the weekly NBC radio program *The Catholic Hour*, which was also broadcast from New York. Over the years, the program's average number of listeners grew to about four million a show. No other Catholic, not even a pope, had been heard by four million people on a weekly basis for two decades in a row.

Though it was a lot of work (and travel, as he would shuttle back and forth from Washington to New York every week), Fulton was up to the task, and his enthusiasm never waned. He had to be hospitalized twice for overwork, but the moment he felt he was well enough (he never liked to convalesce very long), he would get right back to preaching, teaching, evangelizing, and defending the faith at both the university and on the radio.

He began writing books, too, by putting his lectures down on paper in an easy-to-read format. He sometimes produced two or three in a given year. They were translated into multiple languages and helped to make him known all over the world. It was during this time, after he had become a famous priest, apologist, and evangelizer, that Fulton Sheen extended his gracious offer of a quality education to his niece.

2

NEW YORK, NEW YORK

Charity is a quality of the soul rather than an isolated good deed.

—Fulton J. Sheen, *From the Angel's Blackboard*

My uncle had been a young student, living and studying abroad, when he first met the family that I would later stay with in New York City. They had become good friends by the time they heard of my uncle's plans for me, and they kindly offered to let me live with them so that I wouldn't need to board at the school. (Years later I *would* board there, but by then I was a high school junior.) This kind couple also had a niece around my age, who was staying with them. Her name was Maryann, and she was from Nashville, Tennessee. When I arrived in New York City, I was immediately welcomed by a second family. Over the years that's really what they became for me.

Saint Walburga's Academy

My uncle had been right about my school, Saint Walburga's Academy. It was located in Upper Manhattan on West 140th Street and Riverside Drive (it has since moved to Rye, New York). It was wonderful, just as he had said it would be. The upper floors of the beautiful Gothic Revival building, which opened in 1913, had views of the Hudson River, and it is now on the National Register of Historic Places.

The Holy Child sisters were excellent teachers. My French teacher used the immersion method. She would speak only French to us and would take us to French films and restaurants. My uncle heartily approved of her teaching style, and he had a special fondness for France and the French language, which he spoke fluently. Lourdes, France, where Saint Bernadette had visions of the Virgin Mary, was his favorite pilgrimage site in the world.

I had so much fun at Saint Wallburga's that the days just flew by. I did get into trouble once. I can't remember what I did wrong (maybe I talked in the library; schools were much stricter than they are now), but I'll never forget what a nun said to me because of it: "How could you do a thing like that with saint's blood running through your veins?" I was horrified and thought, "That's a terrible thing to say to me!"

Now I realize that the nun was prophetic, but at the time I didn't think of my uncle as a saint. I saw him as a good man and a good priest, and even a holy person. But to me saints were people I read about in books. They were long-dead historical figures. I learned about them in church, or even studied them in school, but I didn't apply the title of "saint" to a living, breathing person I knew in real life. At least I didn't when I was young.

Famous Fulton

I also didn't think of my uncle as famous, because he never acted as though he was. Of course the nuns always made a big fuss over him. Whenever he visited the school, the nuns would fly about, wanting to accommodate him. I thought the special treatment was because he was a priest, not because he was a famous priest.

Strangers came up to my uncle on the street whenever we went walking around the city together. It seemed everyone in New York knew who he was, yet I didn't see this as evidence of his notoriety. I just thought people were very friendly.

Sometimes people came right up to his face to tell him how horrible they thought he was! He didn't mind. He welcomed the interaction. And more often than not, the person would walk away with his opinion of him changed. He truly cared about people, and he showed that by really listening to them. He showed respect for people, even when they were not respectful to him.

As he and I were walking down the street, a man came up to my uncle and was just dreadful. He said things like, "You're a fraud. The priests and the Church are teaching the wrong things to people!" He went on and on, and my uncle didn't say a word. Finally, after the man had said his piece, my uncle said, "I think we ought to get together and discuss this further." He wrote his phone number on a scrap of paper and gave it to him, inviting him to call "because we have to discuss these topics". The man was very taken aback, and he later met with my uncle many times. It turned out he was a fallen-away Catholic who had had some problem with a priest. My uncle told me afterward, "See? There was a soul saved. But if I had been disrespectful to him, he wouldn't have met with me."

The man responded positively to my uncle because he listened to him sympathetically. "The foundation of all true sympathy," he said, "and that which makes it universal, is love." In showing sympathy he did not act in a condescending manner. "The Lord bade us to have sympathy with all people, not in the way of condescension," he said, "but as people touching to heal, as people hating the sin, and loving the sinner."

Weekends with Uncle

I spent every weekend with my uncle. We would meet up in the mornings, and the first place he always took me on Saturdays was Saint Jean Baptiste Church on Seventy-Seventh Street and Lexington Avenue, for confession. Not mine—his.

"Why do you have to go to confession?" I used to ask him. "You can't be a sinner!"

He said that all priests needed to go to regular confession—some even went once a week, as he did. Going frequently, he said, was a good way to receive graces from God.

That sounded pretty good to me. "Can I go with you?" I asked him. But of course, I couldn't go with him *in* the confessional. Confessions are private! I also found out later that his confessor's particular assignment was to hear the confessions of other priests.

After he prayed, sometimes we would take a walk around the church and he would tell me which saints the statues represented. He would do this at any church we stopped at, actually, and I became familiar with a lot of saints.

If there was a statue or a painting or a stained glass window of the Blessed Mother, he would always point it out. He had a great devotion to her. He would tell me she was very important in the life of Christ and should therefore be important in the life of Christians. In his book about her, *The World's First Love: Mary, Mother of God*, he wrote,

"Let those that think that the Church pays too much attention to Mary give heed to the fact that Our Blessed Lord Himself gave ten times as much of His life to her as He gave to His Apostles."

He advised me to feel free to turn to Mary whenever I was in need, as she could understand any sort of problem a woman could have. Over time I came to see how much he believed that Mary "is the one whom every man loves when he loves a woman—whether he knows it or not. She is what every woman wants to be when she looks at herself. She is the way every woman wants to command respect and love because of the beauty of her goodness of body and soul."

After confession, my uncle would typically take me to a rectory where he would catch up with other priests he knew. I had many a lunch and a dinner in different rectories around the city. And if my uncle had a Mass or was booked to give a talk at, say, Saint Patrick's Cathedral or the Church of Saint Agnes on East Forty-Third Street, I would accompany him there and sit with the congregation. I would listen to his talk or attend the Mass, and afterward, we would go out to eat.

On Good Fridays he would speak on the seven last words of Christ. Sometimes he would repeat his talk and speak for three hours straight so that the crowds coming and going might all get a chance to hear as much of the talk as possible. The church would be so packed that the crowd would spill onto the sidewalk. The church had speakers set up outside so that my uncle could be heard on the street.

On days like that I would sit in the church for the whole three hours. I would meet him afterward and go out for a walk or for a visit or for a meal. Then we would return to the church together for his next three-hour talk (he typically spoke from noon to three o'clock and then from six to nine in the evening). Even though I spent six hours on a Saturday sitting in a church pew, I never felt restless. It was a normal way for me to spend an afternoon, and it didn't bother me at all.

With this kind of upbringing (including going to a convent school), the Catholic faith became a part of me. Going to church became almost as regular to me as washing my hands. I still go to daily Mass.

But my childhood wasn't all church all the time. My uncle wanted to be sure I didn't miss out on the fun that also made life—well, worth living.

When he asked me if there was any movie I was interested in seeing, I said I would really like to see *Snow White*. I had heard all of these advertisements for it and had become very intrigued.

"All right," he said, "we'll go." It made him happy to make me happy.

And boy, was I ever happy to see *Snow White*. It was playing at Radio City Music Hall, and I thought it was the grandest place I had ever been.

He also took me to the ice-skating rink at Radio City. Afterward we would go to Rumpelmayer's, the café where well-to-do New Yorkers took their children after a visit to the theatre or the zoo. It was located in the Saint Moritz Hotel on Central Park South, and it was a child's dream, with lots of pink stuffed animals on shelves and European pastries openly displayed in tiers. Patrons were trusted to take only one item, but I always wondered, "If I took two, would they know?"

As we sat there enjoying our dessert, my uncle would say, "Aren't you blessed that you are able to sit here and have a pastry with me? Think of all the people who don't get the chance to enjoy something like this." He said things like that to help me to appreciate such treats, but even though he was a preacher, he was never preachy, so to speak. I found I learned things just from being with him.

He really loved sweets, but he wasn't supposed to eat them. Still, we would go into a Schraft's (a famous chain of tea rooms at the time that served sandwiches, candy, and ice cream) and get this delicious coconut candy with a chocolate bottom (my uncle was partial to chocolate). Then we would stroll down Madison Avenue eating the candy. People would stop him, of course, and he would give them a religious medal or something. He made sure always to carry medals in his pocket. It just didn't dawn on me that it was unusual that seemingly all of New York knew my uncle.

I'm sure his fame also had something to do with the ballet school he chose for me. Back home I had been taking ballet. In fact, my parents had signed me up for lessons at a rather prestigious school. Although I was never going to become a professional dancer, I really enjoyed ballet. To me, it was mostly about fun, but I eventually was good enough to audition for the program that the company was going to perform at the Chicago Theatre during Christmastime. And I won the lead part!

"Of course you have to keep up your ballet when you move to New York," my uncle had insisted. After he asked around and did a little investigating, he enrolled me in the School of American Ballet, which had been cofounded by the renowned Russian choreographer George Balanchine. The prestige of the school didn't mean anything to me at the time, but it was an unbelievable opportunity. My uncle was so proud.

Sometimes when he was entertaining visitors he would take out his phonograph and ask me to dance. He would say, "She goes to the School of American Ballet," and look on, beaming, as I performed. He thought that everybody would think I was as great as he did and that they would be impressed with my dancing. I don't think they were, but dance I did, whenever he asked. After I became a teenager, and other school activities became more interesting to me than dance, I hung up my ballet shoes for good.

Famous Friends

Alfred E. Smith, the former four-time governor of New York, was a very good friend of my uncle. It was a well-known fact that Mr. Smith was a practicing Roman Catholic (and historians cite anti-Catholic prejudice as one of the reasons he lost the presidential election to Herbert Hoover in 1928). We would frequently go to his apartment for dinner and see the sights with him and his wife, Catherine. At the time I didn't realize that Smith was such an important person. I only knew that he was a kind and generous man.

A newspaper once published a photo of Al Smith, his wife, and me coming out of the Empire State Building. My uncle is in the photo, but he's behind us. All that can be seen of him is the top of his face—his forehead and his eyes—over Al Smith's shoulder. The photo illustrates that whenever we were out together, he had me right up in front with him all the time. (My mother was unhappy with the state of my knees in the photograph. Truthfully, they did look a little dirty. I'm not even sure how they got that way. Perhaps from all that kneeling in churches?)

I was a rather agreeable child. Wherever my uncle wanted me to go, I willingly went, always up for the adventure. My eagerness pleased my uncle, who often told me, "You know, you always adapt to any situation."

One time we went to Florida together. He had been sick, and his doctor prescribed a trip south for a change of climate. When I had a break from school, we flew down. While in Florida, we visited with the famous broadcaster and journalist Walter Winchell.

Like my uncle, Winchell first became famous on the radio during the thirties. Also like my uncle, he had a listening audience of millions, although what really shot Mr. Winchell to fame was his coverage of the Lindbergh kidnapping. The story of the twenty-month-old son of an American aviation hero snatched from his crib and held for ransom captivated the country. The story went on for months, almost like the installments of a serial drama. The ransom was paid, but the child was not returned. Later a child's body was found, and later still, a man found in possession of the ransom money (Bruno Hauptmann) was arrested, charged, and prosecuted for kidnapping and murder. As the story progressed to its bitter end, millions of Americans tuned into Walter Winchell, trusting him to keep them up to date on all the details as they unfolded.

It helped that Winchell's staccato style of delivering the news was very distinct. His voice had a sense of urgency that (coupled with the sound effect of a tapping telegraph key) made listeners feel that the news they were hearing was truly up to the minute. It would also be put to good use years later as the narrator for the classic television show *The Untouchables.*

But aside from being a newsman, Walter Winchell was also a very powerful gossip—the first to have a nationally syndicated newspaper column. He was feared by Hollywood stars and political figures alike. Secrets weren't secrets long around Walter Winchell. He just had a way of finding things out about people. Happily, he never gossiped about my uncle. Of course, that's because there was nothing to gossip about.

When I got back home to New York, I remember people asking me what I did during my break. I said,

"My uncle and I sat on a beach with a man named Walter Winchell." When the adults heard this, they were impressed. The other children were more like me. They really didn't know who Walter Winchell was—nor did they care.

Sometimes people—mostly strangers—would come up to me and say, "I met a cousin of yours," and name some person or location where I didn't have any family members (to my knowledge).

"I don't have a cousin there," I would say.

"Oh yes, you do," they would insist.

At times it seemed I had "relatives" coming out of the woodwork. I complained to my uncle about it. "All these people keep finding cousins who aren't cousins."

He waved it away. "Just ignore them," he said. But he didn't mind. Whenever people came up to him claiming to be relatives of relatives he just nodded and welcomed them into the fold. He "adopted" them all.

When I was twelve we went to California. My uncle had it all arranged. "You're going to stay with Irene Dunne and her husband," he informed me. And I thought, "Oh! At last, someone I know!" She was, after all, a movie star.

Irene Dunne was not just a beautiful movie star; she was a great actress (so good that she was nominated a total of five times for an Academy Award). She was perhaps most famous for her films *Love Affair* and *I Remember Mama* and for the three hit films in which she co-starred with Cary Grant (they had amazing chemistry together and were always cast as man and wife).

She was also a practicing Catholic who was a generous contributor to charitable causes. She was a member of the Catholic Motion Picture Guild and the Los Angeles Archdiocesan Council of Catholic Women. Like my uncle, she was quite a fundraising powerhouse, too, raising money for the American Heart Association, the American Red Cross, the American Cancer Society, and Saint John's Hospital in Santa Monica.

In 1949 the University of Notre Dame named her the recipient of their Laetare Medal, which is considered the most prestigious award that an American Catholic can receive. It is given to those "whose genius has ennobled the arts and sciences, illustrated the ideals of the Church and enriched the heritage of humanity".

Dunne's good friend and fellow Catholic, the award-winning actress Loretta Young, invited us to a big dinner party during our visit, and I met other stars that evening. Loretta was a stunningly glamorous woman. She loved fashion, and later in life she married a famous, sought-after designer of stunning gowns, Jean Louis. But even with all her glittering sophistication, she could be very humble and sweet, and she, too, gave generously to charities, including a home for unwed mothers and the Damian Food Fund for the Poor.

Young was a big fan of my uncle's, but she had *her* television show before he had his! (And this wasn't until years after our visit, anyway.) *The Loretta Young Show* ran from 1953 to 1961 and was an anthology series that she produced and hosted, and in which she played a variety of roles. The stories all had moral lessons, and at the end of each episode Young would give a short talk about the story and often quoted from the Bible to make her point. She won three Emmys for it during its run.

Other stars I got to meet included Jim and Marian Jordan, a married couple who were famous radio stars better known as Fibber McGee and Molly. I was very excited to see them in person since my whole family regularly listened to their show. The popular comedy program, which ran for more than twenty years (1935–1959), featured the characters of Fibber (who was just that, a teller of tall tales), his long-suffering wife, Molly, and their fellow townspeople of the fictional Wistful Vista. It was good, clean family fun.

What made meeting the Jordans even more special to us was that they too were originally from Peoria. Jim was the son of a farmer, and Marian was the daughter of a coal miner. They were not only also Catholic, but met in church—singing in the choir.

The star I was most thrilled to meet was Shirley Temple, probably because she was a child, as I was, yet as big a Hollywood star as could be. Not that she acted like it. I was touring a set when we were introduced, and she was a polite, well-behaved, rather normal girl in person. Still, with her dimpled cheeks and golden, corkscrew curls she was an icon. And today she is still seen as the quintessential child star, the gold standard against which all other child stars are measured. She was a triple treat: she could sing, dance, and act—in both comedy and drama—and at the height of her career she was the biggest box-office draw in the nation.

Before leaving California, my uncle and I stayed in Burlingame, south of San Francisco, on a beautiful estate that belonged to some friends of his. The owners were away, but they had given my uncle permission to use their home. He was actually out of the house for most of the day, giving a retreat for priests. But since there were domestics working on the premises, I had adult supervision that allowed me to stay there during the day. I spent my afternoons swimming in the big pool and taking tennis lessons on the tennis court on the grounds. Every day my uncle would call me at some point to tell me how many priests he was bringing over for dinner so that I could inform the cook.

The Priesthood

Whether he was teaching as a professor, speaking as a broadcaster, celebrating the sacraments, or writing books, Sheen was always wholeheartedly involved in what he was doing. This is because all of these actions and abilities shared one thing in common: they were all tied to his priesthood, and he was nothing if not fully a priest.

He loved every aspect of his vocation, from the clothes he had to wear to the responsibilities he had to shoulder. He also wrote books on the subject, *The Priest Is Not His Own* and *Those Mysterious Priests*, as well as books on the Mass and the sacraments. He poured much time, effort, and prayer into giving retreats for priests throughout his life. His identity could not be separated from his priesthood. He lived the vocation, both in its comforts and in its sacrifices, to the full.

Spiritual Fatherhood

In his book *The Priest Is Not His Own*, Sheen explained that priests are not called "Father" carelessly. Although they take a vow of celibacy and are not to have relations with women, they were still responsible for "begetting" children—at least in a spiritual sense. In fact, it was mandatory that they do so. It was part of their "job description". And if they failed to do this, when it came time for them to stand before the Lord's judgment seat, they would have to answer for that when the Lord asked them where their offspring were.

"Whom have you begotten in Christ?" God will ask the priest, Sheen wrote, adding, "Woe to those who are barren! When Our Lord comes looking for the fruit of our fatherhood, we must not be as the barren fig tree, which merits only a curse."

One way of begetting spiritual children was by seeking out and bringing back fallen-away Catholics. It was "the shepherd's primary duty," Sheen wrote, "to search out the lost sheep and stay with it once found." But a priest was called, like Christ, not only to be a shepherd, but also (again, like Christ) to be "the lamb who is offered in caring for them". A priest had to be a victim, Sheen insisted, in order to resemble Christ. It was the only way the Lord would know a priest when his soul appeared at the time of his death, because the priest would look like Christ in heart and soul, the way family members resemble each other.

Sheen felt that the failure to promote sacrifice from both those studying to be priests and those who were already priests was "one reason for the lack of vocations". Priests, Sheen worried, were too comfortable. They were like a person living on the top floor of a two-story home. Below them lived a poor family, suffering from physical, financial, and emotional hardships, and "through intermittent acts of charity [priests] descend to their misery from time to time and relieve it; but ... go back right away to the comfort of [their] lodging." It was "not so with Christ, the Priest. When He went into the depths of human suffering and sin, He never went back—not until all of its misery and guilt were relieved." It was a standard he held himself up to when searching for the lost sheep God called him to recover.

Confession

Christian ministers can lead prayer services, officiate at weddings, and baptize people, but it is the Roman Catholic priest alone who through his ordination and the anointing of his hands is able to offer the Mass and to absolve a person of his sins in God's name. A Catholic cannot receive the Eucharist if he knows himself to be in a state of mortal sin. He must first confess his sins, resolve to sin no more, and be absolved—have his spiritual slate wiped clean.

Wounded pride or deep shame for one's sins often prevents a person from taking advantage of the Sacrament of Reconciliation, and he can end up staying away from the Church for years—decades even—while falling further and further from the faith and its practices. For Sheen, the way to convince a lapsed Catholic to return was often as simple–or as difficult—as persuading him to enter a confessional. In his autobiography, *Treasure in Clay*, he shared some episodes where, through the grace of God, he managed to do that.

While staying in a boardinghouse in Paris, Sheen had a shocking encounter with the woman who ran the place. She showed him a small bottle of poison and explained (through translators) that she intended to kill herself. She had no reason to live, she told him, because her husband had abandoned her, her daughter had become a streetwalker, and she herself could barely make ends meet. She then asked him if he could help her in any way.

"Not if you intend to take that stuff," he told her. But he asked her to put off her planned suicide for a period of nine days. He chose nine days in order to pray a novena (a prayer said every day for a stretch of nine days) to the Sacred Heart of Jesus, telling God, "If you really love souls—and you do—then save this one." As he prayed he came to realize that, as a baptized Catholic, the woman could receive the grace to go on if she would but humble herself and confess her sins and ask for forgiveness.

The night before the novena ended, Sheen persuaded the woman to go to confession. She did, and there she "received the gift of faith". A joyous Sheen was able to give her Communion the following day. Her return to the fold was not the only result of the novena: she was later reunited with her husband and daughter, and the three of them became known as a model Catholic family in their village.

When Sheen was staying in Saint Patrick's Catholic Church in London, England, early one morning as he opened its doors, a young woman slumped inside. She looked to be in her early twenties and in need of sobering up after a long night of drinking. Sheen offered her tea and asked her name. When he heard it, he pointed to a billboard that stood across the street, advertising a musical that was currently playing in the theatre. "Is that you?" he asked. The woman admitted that she was, in fact, the leading lady in the show. Seeing she wanted help, Sheen asked her to return once she had sobered up some more, but before the matinee, so that they could talk. She agreed on one condition: that he promise not to ask her to go to confession. He promised.

Later that afternoon, she came as per their agreement. He gave her a tour of the church, and as they passed by the confessional Sheen gave her a little shove. As he promised, he did not ask her to go—he just pushed her inside! Years later, when she was professed as a nun, Sheen presented her with her veil.

3

A PROPER EDUCATION

One of the most practical ways of assuring that we will always have enough is to give and give and give in the name of the Lord. Similarly, the most rapid increase in love of God can be obtained by being totally generous with our neighbors

—Fulton J. Sheen, *From the Angel's Backboard*

One thing my uncle always taught me was how to behave in public. He was such a proper person. People sometimes said that he was vain. That comment always bothered me because it simply wasn't true. He always said that he was an ambassador for Christ and that as such he should look right. Nowadays casual clothes are the norm. But during his era, people dressed up if they were going out in public.

He often repeated, "You have to always look proper." And this is ingrained in me to this day. Recently I was invited down to Palm Beach and West Palm Beach for events commemorating my uncle. When I accepted the invitation, I remember saying to my daughter, "I have to get a couple of nice dresses."

My daughter said, "You have a lot of nice pantsuits." But I knew those wouldn't do. My daughter argued, "The secretary of state [Hillary Clinton at the time] goes all over the world in pantsuits, and you can't go to a religious event in a pantsuit?"

"No," I said. "I have to wear a dress." That's how I was raised.

I remember one time when my uncle took me shopping for dresses. We went to Altman's, a luxury department store on Fifth Avenue, and he asked the first salesgirl he saw, "What size do you think she would she wear?"

She looked me over and told him a size. He promptly marched over to a rack of dresses in that size and selected six of them.

The salesgirl opened her eyes wide. "Isn't she going to try them on?"

My uncle shook his head as he fished for his wallet. "Oh, they'll fit!"

And they did!

Another time we went shopping at FAO Schwarz, the oldest toy store in the United States. He bought me a skating skirt and white ice skates with what looked like fur cuffs around them. I loved them so much that once I grew out of them I couldn't bear to throw them out. I'm glad I saved them, because years later my daughter was able to wear them.

My uncle loved red, and when he spotted a red coat my size, he insisted, "You've got to get this red coat!" Years later when my daughter was a little girl, he took her shopping and bought her a red coat with a black velvet collar. And then, when she had a little girl of her own, she bought a red coat for her, too. It has become a family tradition.

Speaking of red and propriety, I had to learn all the identifying colors of clerical attire. In those days priests didn't wear secular clothing, and even today, the color of the zucchettos (the yarmulke-like caps priests wear) and sashes of a monsignor differs from the colors worn by a bishop and a cardinal. A monsignor wears a sort of dark pink shade, a bishop wears purple, and a cardinal, of course, wears bright red.

I also had to learn the proper titles for members of the clergy so that when my uncle introduced me to any of them I would know what to say. A monsignor is simply called "Monsignor", a bishop is called "Your Excellency", and a cardinal is addressed as "Your Eminence".

Unless he introduced me, people didn't always know that I was Fulton Sheen's niece, because I never called him "uncle". He never said not to call him uncle; I just addressed him properly. At first everyone called him "Father", then it was "Monsignor", and finally "Bishop". I just followed along. I never did call him "Your Excellency", but I otherwise tended to follow what other people were saying. In fact, even when I speak of him now, even when recalling a childhood memory, I usually refer to him as "the bishop". (Before he died he was given the title of archbishop, but he had retired by then.)

When I was about to meet the apostolic delegate, the pope's ambassador to the United States, my uncle told me, "Now you must remember his name: Amleto Giovanni Cicognani." I kept saying it over and over to myself. To this day I have not forgotten it. The funny thing is, I never needed to use it. I had bothered to memorize the whole thing, but even if my uncle had introduced me to him, I would never have needed to call the apostolic delegate by his whole name!

A Detached Spirit

My uncle made friends wherever he went. Salespeople loved him. People often wanted to give him things for free, and sometimes when I was with him, they wanted to give things to me.

When we would go to the milliner's, for instance, one of the designers almost always gave me a hat as a gift. In those days both men and women often wore hats. My uncle typically wore a homburg. I will never forget his size: long, oval. After my uncle passed on, I kept one of his homburgs. And one time, one of my grown sons decided to try it on. It didn't fit. "I guess you're not a long, oval!" I laughed.

It made me feel funny, sometimes, to receive gifts from strangers. When I expressed my uneasiness to my uncle, he told me not to worry. He knew that people were pleased to give us things and that our refusal of their kindness would insult them. He told me to accept the gifts whenever they were given but "always do so with a detached spirit. That way if you lose it or give it away, or if it gets destroyed somehow, it won't matter."

This was exactly the way my uncle lived. He had a lot of possessions but was always giving, giving, giving. He became famous for giving his possessions away. If a visitor picked up anything off of his mantel and admired it, for example, he would say, "Take it home." After a while, friends and relatives who gave him a gift knew not to expect to see it in his home the next time they visited. He would most likely have given it away by then!

He knew as many poor people as wealthy people, and he treated them all the same. Because he showed everyone the same respect, I was unaware of the class differences between his friends who lived on Fifth Avenue and those who lived in the Bronx. When people were joining us for dinner, he never said things like, "Oh, this person is wealthy and important, so be on your best behavior." No. He thought everybody was equally important—and I was always supposed to be on my best behavior anyway, whether we had guests, of any class, or not.

My uncle's generous reputation preceded him, and often people came right up to him on the street and asked him for money. He never refused them, even when I suspected that they weren't being honest about their needs and were taking advantage of my uncle. Sometimes I would ask, "What if that person's not telling the truth?"

His reply was always the same: "I can't take that chance."

My father, too, worried that my uncle gave away too much of his money and possessions. But my uncle believed in the spiritual rewards for generosity. "Throw bread on the water," he would tell my father, "and it comes back angel cake."

A Man for the People

My uncle really tried to live by the words of Jesus: "You shall love the Lord your God with all your heart, and with all your soul, and with all your mind. This is the great and first commandment. And a second is like it, You shall love your neighbor as yourself. On these two commandments depend all the law and the prophets" (Mt 22:37–40). He once wrote:

I am loved by God despite all my faults, failures, and infidelities. . . . The least I can do for others is to do what God has done for me. Once I no longer regard myself as a superman, who refuses to share the struggle of others, then when others are weak, I am weak; when they are poor, I am poor; when they are tearful, my cheeks are damp. . . .

Only when I am as weak and helpless as my neighbor can I help him. Then there is no spirit of judgement, no sense of superiority, no superciliousness, no looking down one's nose at others. I am his companion in repentance. I too am waiting for grace.

His charity knew no bounds. He was attentive to others wherever he went.

I would accompany my uncle to the studio where NBC produced *The Catholic Hour*, a Sunday-night radio show. It featured different guest speakers on serious, timely subjects, and my uncle often hosted the program.

The shows were taped in front of a live audience. There were a number of people—I guess you could call them fans of my uncle—who tried to attend every taping. After a while I got to know some of the "regulars". My uncle thought it was important for me to be friendly toward them and get to know them.

Once he especially instructed me to acquaint myself with a man who had leprosy. His face was sadly disfigured, and it frightened some of the other people in the audience, who took pains to avoid him. My uncle said to me, "You have to go over and talk to him because no one speaks to him. Don't worry. He's not contagious." So I obediently went over to the man, introduced myself, and sat down next to him. After a few tapings I grew so accustomed to his appearance that he looked really quite normal to me. We got to know each other quite well and had some great chats. I met a lot of interesting people through my uncle.

Another interesting person was the Jewish shopkeeper who was a friend of my uncle. Whenever my uncle would put out a call to his listeners to donate toward the missions, he would encourage people to "send anything"—a nickel, a penny, a dime, old jewelry—to help feed the hungry of the world. A lot of old Irish ladies would send my uncle their chains, rings, and earrings (usually the jewelry wasn't that expensive), and the shopkeeper would give my uncle money in trade for them. Truthfully, most of the jewelry was inexpensive, and my uncle knew that the shopkeeper would give him more money than the items were actually worth. That was his secret way of donating to the missions, too.

When I asked my uncle why the shopkeeper didn't convert to Catholicism, he replied simply, "He was never given the gift of faith."

Until then I hadn't realized that faith was a gift from God. My uncle had a number of friends of different faiths. He never pushed Catholicism on them. Instead he lived by his faith. And I think they all profited by his example and friendship. In fact, the shopkeeper was given the gift of faith eventually. He accepted Christianity on his deathbed, and he was baptized just before he passed away.

Guidance Counselor

My uncle could make friends anywhere. Once while riding in a hospital elevator, the operator told him, "Bishop Sheen, there's a nurse here who's been dying to find a priest to talk to. She's not a Catholic, but she's engaged to a doctor who's a very, very observant Catholic. She's concerned about how their religious differences could affect their marriage and has been trying to find somebody who can help them. Can you recommend someone?"

My uncle didn't miss a beat. "Is she on duty?"

"Yes."

"What floor is she on? Take me to her."

After hearing the nurse's story, my uncle said to her, "I don't think you're going to have a problem, but I think the best thing for you two to do, is to come and see me."

The couple went to see him many times and he advised them. She eventually became a Catholic, and my uncle, of course, officiated at their wedding. He later baptized their children. They were a beautiful family.

As I said earlier, my uncle knew that unless God gave someone the gift of faith, that person would not be converted by anything he could say. But if my uncle believed that the seed of faith had been planted in someone's heart, he would get to work watering and nurturing that seed. He took very seriously his responsibility to evangelize others. Once he set out to help someone to convert, he didn't hand that person over to colleagues. He took care of him himself.

He also liked to play matchmaker. One time, when my uncle was national director of the Society for the Propagation of the Faith, he had the idea of matching up a lovely young woman who worked part-time for him with a man just her age who also came from a nice, devout family. He introduced them with hopes of making a love match.

They dated a bit, but it didn't work out. At first my uncle was disappointed. But then the young woman told him that she wanted to be a nun. That changed everything. "I'm not sure what order to join," she confessed. "I'm looking into a few of them."

"Oh, no, no, no." As far as my uncle was concerned, there was only one choice. "You have to be a Holy Child nun!"

And that's exactly what she became—and still is. (And not to worry, my uncle found someone else for the young man to marry!)

My uncle never pushed a religious vocation on me. He enjoyed it when in my senior year of high school I told him about my goal to be invited to every prom at the boys' schools. Whenever I would visit him he would ask, "How are you doing on your 'project'?" (Actually, I didn't do too badly!)

But my uncle was loyal to the Holy Child sisters from the first time he met them in England. He often said that the general aim of education is to train the whole person: "It should not only perfect the mind, but also build character." When he toured one of the Holy Child schools, he observed that the sisters were very good at giving their students such a foundation.

After he returned to the States, he contacted the order here and began actively supporting it. He ran retreats for the sisters and eventually set up scholarships at their schools. He also made sure to attend every graduation he could, and so, of course, he came to mine.

When I was old enough to start looking at colleges, my uncle told me, "You're not going to have to look; you're going to Rosemont College." Located near Philadelphia, Rosemont was a Catholic liberal arts college for women. And guess who founded and ran the school? The Holy Child sisters, of course.

Converts

Because he spoke about the faith so well on the radio, Sheen was inundated with letters from listeners asking for instruction. Unwilling to refuse all the sheep the Lord sent to him, Sheen arranged to teach them in "convert classes" on Saturdays in New York City, where he would also preach the Mass the following day, often at either Saint Patrick's Cathedral or the Church of Saint Paul the Apostle. His lesson plans consisted of twenty-five hours of instruction, which he considered the minimum before a person was ready to be received into the Church.

His colleagues at the university—while no doubt admiring his tireless work for the Lord—predicted that he would die before the age of forty-five. They were wrong, but he did require hospitalization for exhaustion more than once. As Joan has said, he did not discriminate, and his many converts ran the gamut of backgrounds from statesmen to homeless men. All were equal in the eyes of God, he knew.

Clare Boothe Luce

Because of her stature as a congressman, an ambassador, and a writer, however, Clare Boothe Luce is one of his most well-known catechumens. Sheen invited Luce to dinner soon after the death of her daughter, Ann, who died in a car accident in 1944. When in conversation he touched on the goodness of God, she grew incensed. God is not good, she said, because he had taken her daughter's life when she was just nineteen. Sheen challenged her, saying that she could come to know Christ and his Church through her sorrow. Intrigued, Luce submitted to instruction with Sheen and entered the Church two years later.

Luce had "a mind like a rapier", Sheen said, adding that she was the most brilliant person he had ever instructed. She became a lifelong friend of Sheen and a prominent public defender of Catholicism.

Victor, the Leper

Another convert who became a lifelong friend of Sheen was a homeless leper named Victor. Once Sheen heard about Victor, and how he had been thrown out of his home when his parents found out about his disease, Sheen wanted to help him right away. But it took six months to track him down. Once he did, he made sure that Victor received medical attention. He helped him to find a place to live and had him over for dinner every Friday night. Sheen counseled him to overcome his resentment and hatred toward his parents and his disease and, of course, instructed him in the faith. He became a close friend whom Joan would later meet.

Sheen told a funny story about a self-important woman who once visited him, claiming that she wanted to become a Catholic. As an intellectual, she said, she could not be taught by just any priest. She wanted him to teach her, and would he do so—making sure to "intellectualize" his faith for her? Sheen said that he was willing to teach anyone who came to him, including the leper who a few moments before had occupied the chair she was sitting on. She bolted from the room and he never saw her again.

Bella Dodd

A New York City lawyer and a Communist, Bella Dodd served as legal counsel to the Communist Party when it was being investigated by the House Un-American Activities Committee in the 1950s. Senator J. Howard McGrath of Rhode Island either saw the spark of faith in her or believed that Sheen, with his deep understanding of Communism and his familiarity with the writings of Marx, Lenin, and Stalin, would be able to turn her around. The senator recommended to Dodd that she pay Sheen a call. At first, she could not see why she should—even if he was well versed in the tenets of Communism. It wasn't until the senator intimated that perhaps she was afraid to see Sheen that she decided to visit him.

It didn't take long for her to crack. After making polite small talk, Sheen observed aloud that she looked unhappy and suggested that she enter the chapel with him to say a prayer. They knelt in silence and she was soon in tears. "Touched by grace," Sheen said. Shortly thereafter, he accepted her as his student, taught her the faith, and brought her into the fold. She later became a prominent and active anti-Communist Catholic.

Louis Budenz

Another famous Communist, Louis Budenz, was the editor of the *Daily Worker*, the party's newspaper, and a spy for the Soviet Union. He wrote pieces that personally attacked Sheen, who was one of the loudest, but also one of the sanest and most intelligent, American voices against Communism.

After reading every argument Budenz wrote against him, Sheen wrote a response that he had published in pamphlet form and distributed. People would use it to refute Budenz point by point in public squares. Everywhere Budenz turned, he heard Sheen, read Sheen, or encountered someone using Sheen against him. It got to the point where Budenz wouldn't allow his family to listen to the radio when he knew Sheen would be on the air. The priest had become the bane of his existence. Yet the Central Committee of the Communist Party thought Budenz would be the perfect representative of theirs to meet with Sheen and attempt to convert him to their side. It would have been a huge triumph to "get Sheen". But it was not Sheen who would convert.

Sheen agreed to meet Budenz, and when he did he surprised the man by immediately cutting off any talk of Communism. He told him that he didn't want to discuss politics, but rather Budenz's soul. This shook Budenz, who had grown up Catholic, to the core. He would leave soon afterward and not see Sheen for another six or seven years, but that whole space of time he would be haunted by the statement. When he finally asked to see Sheen again, it would be to take secret instruction in the Catholic faith. In 1945 Sheen received Budenz, his wife, and their children into the Church at Saint Patrick's Cathedral, stunning the party when they announced the news to the Associated Press.

Communism

Sheen spoke out against Communism from his early days at Catholic University. At the time, Russia was an ally of the United States, and many believed that its most Communist days were in the past. But Sheen could see with an almost prophet-like understanding that the "specter of communism" was still on the move.

He began sounding the alarm—much to the annoyance of those who disagreed with him (such as President Roosevelt and fellow priests and professors). He was relentless in warning against the dangers of Russia's becoming a superpower, disturbing their collective illusion that Russia was a democracy. Many wished he would just shut up or that somehow he could be proven wrong once and for all. Instead, he broadcast this prediction on the radio: "Pilate and Herod were enemies and became friends over the bleeding body of Christ, so one day communism and Nazism, which are now enemies, will become friends over the bleeding body of Poland." In September 1939 he was sadly proven right when Russia and Germany both invaded Poland and divided the country between them.

Communism, Sheen explained, worked by appealing to people with three main principles that sounded rather Christian on first hearing. The first, that people were called to brotherhood. Second, that in order to accomplish one's mission in life, one must make sacrifices. And third, that the individual had to resign one's will to a higher power. Unfortunately, in the case of Communism, the higher power was not God, but the government, and the sacrifices asked of the people were not made voluntarily.

Sheen went on to argue that Karl Marx, author of the *Communist Manifesto*, wrote that man was a slave to two things, private property and religion, and that both should be destroyed. The problem with this line of thinking was that the rights to own property and to practice the faith of one's choosing are guarantees of freedom, not of slavery. Communism was about creating contradiction, conflict, and ultimately chaos. "He who thinks [Communism] is an economic or political system," Sheen warned, "is ignorant of its nature."

On one episode of his television show, *Life Is Worth Living*, Sheen gave a dramatic reading of a scene from Shakespeare's *Julius Caesar*, in which he changed the names of Caesar, Cassius, Marc Antony, and Brutus to those of Communist leaders Stalin, Beria, Malenkov, and Vishinsky. When in the play they speak of Caesar's death, corpse, and judgment, Sheen made it sound as though they were speaking of Stalin's instead. When the real Stalin had a stroke a few days later, and died four days after that, people were thunderstruck. They were convinced that Sheen was some kind of prophet.

It wasn't the last time he would display his foresight. When Archbishop Karol Wojtyla was elected pope in 1978, Sheen was thrilled and prophesied in his autobiography, "John Paul II will go down in history as one of the great Pontiffs of all times."

The new pope was to Sheen an example of heroic resistance to both Nazi and Communist oppression. During the German occupation of Poland, the Nazis persecuted the Polish Church and closed its seminaries. Thus Wojtyla's priestly formation was conducted in secret. As a priest and a bishop, Wojtyla stood up to the efforts of the atheistic Communist regime to dechristianize the country. As a result, Sheen had hopes for his papacy. He told him in a letter, "I pray for your Holiness as for another Gregory the Great." It was prophetic. John Paul II was referred to as "the Great" by many prominent Catholics immediately after his death in 2005, and he was canonized only nine years later.

4

THREE TO GET MARRIED

*The basic error of humankind has been to assume that only
two are needed for love: you and me, or society and me, or
humanity and me. Really, it takes three: self, other selves,
and God, you, and me, and God.... Love is triune or
it dies. It requires three virtues: faith, hope, and charity,
which intertwine, purify, and regenerate one another.*

—Fulton J. Sheen, *Three to Get Married*

By the time I was in high school, my uncle no longer
needed to go to New York on weekends. I boarded at my
school during the week, and on the weekends I visited my
uncle at his house in Washington, D.C. During my college years at Rosemont, I would bring a friend along with
me so that we could date the young men from Georgetown. We would take the train on Fridays and stay with
my uncle in the house he had had built with his share
of the farm money. The house was more like a rectory
because he had two other priests living with him. They all
taught at Catholic University together.

One of his roommates was rather quiet and kept to
himself. He taught Sanskrit, if I remember correctly. The
other priest was friendly and joked around with us. We

thought he was hysterical when he would tease us about our dates. He was later ordained a bishop.

As in every place my uncle lived, there was a chapel set up in one of the rooms. It was on the ground floor, and the priests said Mass there every morning. When my friends and I stayed over but were tired from dancing the night before, we would jokingly ask the priests to pipe the sounds of the Mass into our room so that we wouldn't need to get up.

Meeting Jerry

On one of these weekends in Washington, one of my friends suggested I go on a blind date with her brother. Jerry Cunningham was attending Georgetown Law School, and when his sister showed me his photograph, I saw a very handsome man wearing a naval officer's uniform. I suppose that means it wasn't really a blind date.

Jerry and I had a wonderful time, and soon we were going steady. Also a devout Catholic, Jerry had no problem with my uncle being a priest or with the fact that when he took me home after our dates, my "home" was a rectory. What made it even funnier was when he walked me to the door, the chapel was straight ahead. Undaunted, he would give me a good-night kiss right in front of it.

At that time my father was encouraging me to go to law school after college. He thought it would be a great direction for me. My uncle, on the other hand, was advising me to find a job and an apartment in Washington. I kept saying, "Yes, yes, I'm thinking about it," to both of them, but I didn't want to follow the advice of either one.

When my uncle met Jerry, he approved of him right away. Not only was Jerry very easygoing, but like my uncle, he had a great sense of humor; they made each other laugh. In no time at all, my uncle learned to love Jerry, and he gave us his blessing when we got engaged in our senior year.

After we graduated in 1949, I went back to Chicago to plan the wedding while Jerry stayed in Washington to study for the bar exam. Since my uncle and husband-to-be were good friends by then, I knew that they would look out for each other. Jerry and I were married on October 29, 1949, and my uncle gave us an autographed copy of his book *Three to Get Married* as a gift.

Because my uncle's house in Washington was where I stayed when I met and dated the man I would marry, I have fond memories of it. At the time it was a pretty average-looking, two-story home. But years later, a very well-known Irishman bought the place and had it entirely renovated. The *Wall Street Journal* ran a story about the house, mentioning that it had once belonged to Fulton Sheen. They printed photos showing a fine *three*-story home complete with a *pool*. I sadly realized that everyone who read the piece—who didn't know my uncle—would mistakenly think that Fulton Sheen had lived the high life.

Sometime later my son and one of his cousins drove to Washington to see the house that had played such an important role in his parents' lives. As the house is situated at the end of a cul-de-sac, the owner noticed them when they stopped the car and got out to take a look. A little suspicious, the Irishman came out and confronted them. When my son explained about his uncle, the man's demeanor changed. "Oh, come in, come in," he said with a brogue.

The man told them the story of how he came to buy the house. He was looking for a home in the area because of his work. When the real-estate agent first showed him the house and told him who the previous owner was, he was unimpressed and went to look at some other places. Afterward, walking by a bookstore, he spotted a book in the window with my uncle's face on it. Fulton Sheen seemed to be staring back at him, and the man wondered if it might be a sign. He called his mother back in Ireland and told her the name of the previous owner, and she immediately said, "You must buy that house!" So he did. He lived there for years before eventually moving back to Ireland.

Apartment Hunting

When Jerry and I were seeking a place of our own, my uncle asked, "Where are you looking for an apartment?"

"Virginia," Jerry said. "All of our friends seem to be moving there. They say the rents are cheaper."

"Let's get together and find you a place," my uncle said. He knew someone who owned an apartment building down the street from his place, and he helped us to get a beautiful apartment there. He even filled it up for us. He arranged to have all our wedding gifts shipped there, and he gave us his extra furniture.

Because he knew just what we needed, when his priest friends asked what they could give us as wedding gifts, he would suggest specific pieces, such as a mirror or something else he thought we could use. Among the many lovely gifts was a lighted Lalique crystal sculpture of the Madonna and Child. My uncle recommended that we always have an extra bulb so that it would always be lighted. It burned for sixty-four years.

What a wonderful surprise Jerry and I had when we got home from our honeymoon. When we walked into our new apartment, we found that everything had been set up for us. I mean everything! There were pictures on the walls and flowers all around. It was beautiful—the loveliest wedding gift of all. The best part (the part that my uncle was proudest of) was that the refrigerator was completely stocked. He had gone food shopping himself and hand-selected all of our groceries (and I think he had a lot of fun doing it, too). As newlyweds we did not have much money, so we were very appreciative of all his thoughtfulness and generosity. But sometimes he was too generous. I kidded him for a long time afterward, saying, "I don't think I'll ever have lamb chops that thick again!"

Married with Children

My uncle loved Christmas. He had both a childlike and a deeply spiritual excitement about it. He said that Christmas was the "discovery of the Missing Link.... Scholars have been concerned about finding man's relationship to the beast. Christmas is the discovery of ... not the link that binds man to beast, but the link that binds man to God. The Divine Babe was the real Cave Man, for He was born in a cave in Bethlehem."

From early on in my married life, Christmas became the time for the Sheen and Cunningham families to gather together. I was the first daughter in my family to marry and have children, and it became the tradition for me to host the family Christmas dinner. Every year I invited my parents, my siblings, and, of course, my uncle over to our place to celebrate.

During the month of December, my uncle enjoyed going to the stores, seeing the decorations, and shopping for presents for other people. When my family expanded to include my five children, he enjoyed shopping all the more—especially for the children. Christmas almost turned him into a child himself. One time he bought two dolls for my daughter, Anne. One was from the Madame Alexander Doll Company, which made collectible dolls with costumes from all over the world and various historical periods. The other was a French doll with a porcelain face. They were such lovely, charming dolls. My daughter still has them.

We would give him presents, too, but it could be hard to know what to get him. Not only were people always giving him presents, but he was always giving them away. One Christmas, when the children were still quite small, I wondered aloud. "What can I get the bishop?"

"Why not give him a train for under his tree?" My children suggested. "We know he doesn't have one of those."

So we did—and he loved it! He got down with the kids and played with them and that train all afternoon. We had such fun.

He appreciated crèches under the tree, too. A woman who helped him sometimes would make the most beautiful Nativity scenes using Italian figurines. Over the years he acquired quite a collection. He gave a number of them to me, and I still put them out at Christmas.

He never could pass up a religious statue. One time when my uncle and I were shopping in New York City, we passed by one of those "Going Out of Business" stores that are never really going out of business. In the window display, my uncle spotted a ceramic rendition of the Last Supper. It had Jesus, the twelve apostles, tiny dishes and wine cruets—everything. But in the same window were all sorts of garish, touristy things. The clash made my uncle gasp. "Oh, look at that, and in this horrible store! We have to buy it!" So we went in and bought it. My uncle pressed the bag into my hand and insisted I take the statue home, so I did.

The following week my uncle and I walked past the same store, and guess what we saw in the window display? Another statue of the Last Supper!

I turned to my uncle and asked, "Are we getting that one, too?"

He learned his lesson!

The Other "Bishop"

Then there was the time he wanted to buy my children a present of a different sort: a dog. I didn't like the idea. "I'm expecting a baby," I protested. I was going to have my third child. "I don't need a dog."

But my uncle persisted. "Well, Joan, the boys [my sons, Francis Jerome and Fulton] should have a dog, and I have been researching breeds to find the best dog. Poodles sound best. They don't shed. They just need trimming. And they're very, very smart."

So buy them a dog he did. A royal-sized standard poodle. And well, I almost died when I caught sight of the size of him. He was huge. It had to duck to go under a table. And he was a *puppy*.

My uncle named him *L'évêque* ("bishop" in French). The dog *was* very smart—and well trained. His trainer instructed us, "Don't ever, ever feed him from the table." And my children didn't. They took the trainer very seriously. They didn't seem to understand that the advice was so that the dog wouldn't learn bad habits. I think they were afraid that the dog would collapse or something.

Everyone ended up loving L'évêque—even our neighbors. Whenever he got a trim we would prance up and down the neighborhood, showing off his new cut and enjoying all the attention he got. He was a wonderful dog. He lived to be thirteen years old.

My uncle thought it was great that the kids had this huge dog. He always got the biggest kick hearing stories about him. For example, one day I found the dog spread-eagle on the floor at the bottom of the stairs. He had foam all over his face. Trembling, I called to my husband, "Jerry! Come quickly! The dog! I don't know what's wrong!"

Then I noticed that my youngest son at the time, Fulton, was sitting next to the dog. He had his pretend shaving kit open and was using its "razor" to "shave" him! The dog wasn't frothing at the mouth; he was slathered in *shaving* foam. Yes, L'évêque was a *very* patient dog, and he always stuck with the youngest child no matter what the child might do.

Priest's Best Friend

My uncle had a dog of his own in Washington: Chumley, an English setter. And this dog he just *loved*. My uncle trained the dog himself, and when people were over for dinner, Chumley would sit by his seat. Before the meal, my uncle would tell Chumley that it was time to say grace, and the dog would put his paws together and bow his head as if in prayer. When giving him treats, my uncle would say, "Chumley! It's Lent! Mortify yourself!" And he would lay a piece of meat on the dog's nose. Chumley would sit very still until my uncle finally said, "Easter!" Then Chumley would snap back to life—and eat the treat.

In Washington, my uncle would let Chumley run in his backyard. It was full of grass and dirt—not very manicured. When my uncle called him inside, he bounded over happily, put his dirty paws on my uncle's clothes, and drooled all over him. My uncle didn't mind. He would pet Chumley and coo over him, no matter how dirty he was.

When my uncle moved to New York City he did not keep a dog (no room for them to run). This was probably why he got L'évêque for my boys. But the move to the city was necessary, since he had been appointed the national director of the Society for the Propagation of the Faith, and its main office was near the Empire State Building. Then, another turn of events would also keep him in the city: he was contracted to broadcast a new television series there. The show was called *Life Is Worth Living*.

The "Prop"

The 1950s were a decade of abundant blessings for Sheen. It started off with his being named national director of the Society for the Propagation of the Faith in 1950. By June of the following year, he was ordained a bishop, and in 1952, he began his television show, *Life Is Worth Living*. His being blessed with the responsibilities of these three special roles could not have been better timed.

Sheen considered the period he served at "the Prop" (as he fondly called it) one of the most joyful of his life. It is an international organization, and Sheen was in charge of its U.S. office, which meant he represented the Church in America at the Sacred Congregation for the Propagation of the Faith in Rome. Basically, it was his job to keep American prayers and money flowing in support of Catholic missions throughout the world, which he did until 1966. He raised millions of dollars.

There was already more than a bit of the missionary in Fulton Sheen. Before he traveled around the country and the world, his words had gone before him, over the radio and on the printed page, enabling him to sow seeds of evangelization in countries long before he ever visited them.

Sheen saw evangelization and teaching as pretty much the same thing. If a person had some sort of special knowledge or expertise, he believed, it was that person's obligation to share it with others. If he did not, then he was no better than a hoarder or a miser. Evangelization is spreading the Good News of Christ's life, death, and Resurrection, and it is the duty of all Christians, but especially of bishops, since they are the successors of the apostles, whom Christ commanded to "go therefore and make disciples of all nations" (Mt 28:19). This command is the Great Commission, the reason missions exist in the first place. It was a command that Sheen did not take lightly.

Before his work for the Prop, and throughout his teaching career, Sheen did mission work in the United States, on weekends or during breaks in the school year, preaching and raising funds so that churches and hospitals could be built in poor areas of the South, in states such as Alabama and Oklahoma.

In 1948 Francis Cardinal Spellman, archbishop of New York, invited Sheen to accompany him on travels to the East Indies, Australia, China, and Japan. At each of these countries great crowds came to greet them. Sheen humbly said that they were there for the cardinal, but he gave most of the speeches, did most of the radio broadcasts, and thus made the biggest impression on the people they met along the way. It was most likely the success of that diplomatic trip that inspired the U.S. bishops to appoint Sheen to direct the Society for the Propagation of the Faith. It was that same trip that also added the first fuel to the fire of what would become Cardinal Spellman's jealousy of Sheen.

Television Star

On June 11, 1951, Sheen was consecrated as an auxiliary bishop in the Archdiocese of New York. Eight months later he began the *Life Is Worth Living* weekly primetime television show. Filmed at the Adelphi Theatre in New York City and broadcast on the Dumont Television Network, the show was not meant to be a religious program (despite its host being dressed in his bishop's regalia); it was rather meant to be an educational and thought-provoking series that elevated and encouraged its viewers to think more deeply about such matters as morality, philosophy, and citizenry. Sheen, being a veteran college professor, presented his subjects in such a way that both intellectuals and the less educated were able to understand him.

Sheen's vocabulary, humor, and style had a little something for everyone, and the show was instantly popular. Within two months, the number of stations carrying his show jumped from three to fifteen. Soon millions of people were regular viewers. In fact, the show became a sort of cultural event that appealed to audiences of all faiths. Viewers, feeling as though they were back in school or in church, often dressed up as if they were going to attend one or the other before sitting down to watch an episode.

Sheen's becoming a television star did not help matters much when it came to the cardinal's jealousy, but it was a big boon to the missions. Though he was contracted for $26,000 an episode, Bishop Sheen never saw the money. It went straight to Rome to be distributed to missionaries throughout the world. For some people, the idea that an American refused to keep such a large, regular paycheck for himself and instead donated it to the poor in other countries, is enough to consider that man a saint.

Bishop Sheen derived great satisfaction knowing that his salary provided a regular means of support for the missions and that he had earned the money in such a positive manner—the edification of his viewers. Adding to his joy was the money his viewers began generously contributing to the Society for the Propagation of the Faith. During many of his shows, Sheen informed his viewers of the suffering endured by those in other countries and asked them directly for help on their behalf. As a result, over time the Society received millions of dollars in donations from American citizens, some who gave a little and others who would go so far as to sacrifice vacation money and nest eggs in order to give to those who had so much less. For that decade, the generosity of Americans was responsible for the building of hundreds of schools, wells, and hospitals in many struggling and underserved countries. Their charity made life more worth living both for the giver, whose spirit was enhanced knowing he had done a good deed for his neighbor, and for the recipient, whose quality of life was much improved through the help of a stranger from far away.

Closer to home, Sheen proved to be a beloved boss to those who worked for him at the Prop, where he developed into a kind of spiritual director to his more than forty employees. He made sure that between fielding calls, sending money to the missions, and wading through his fan mail (at the height of *Life Is Worth Living* he was receiving over twenty-thousand letters a day), they took time to pray the Rosary or to study Scripture together (during his tenure, he claimed, the staff got through nearly all of the books of the Bible). He also enjoyed breaks with them that featured tea, cookies, and lots of laughter.

Milk Money

During Sheen's tenure at the Society for the Propagation of the Faith, the organization was pulling in more money than it ever had in its history. Americans were donating more to the missions than any other country. Aware of this, Cardinal Spellman asked Sheen to give him some of the money for Europeans suffering from postwar food shortages. While a charitable idea, to be sure, Sheen nevertheless refused, arguing that the Society's money was already earmarked for missions in the Third World. The U.S. government was already providing aid to Europe, he said, and too much of the Society's money would go toward delivery expenses. Sheen wanted to use the Society's money according to the purpose of the organization and where it would be the most useful and go the furthest.

Spellman did not take well to being refused, and he saw it as an act of disobedience. There ended up being a lot of correspondence between the two of them about the issue. The more it dragged on, the angrier Spellman became, because Sheen's no was the first no he had ever received in his seventeen years as archbishop of New York. Their disagreement escalated to the point where it made its way to Rome and to the pope. Since priests were always supposed to be obedient to their superiors, Spellman was sure that the pope would agree with him. He was surprised, then, to discover that the pope instead agreed with Sheen that the money should go to the missions.

Two years later a similar situation occurred. This time, Cardinal Spellman wanted monetary reimbursement for a donation of powdered milk that he had made to the Society. Sheen refused, explaining donations are only truly donations if they are freely given without expectation of payment. The milk had not been purchased from Spellman (neither had Spellman purchased it; the milk had been given to the archdiocese, to be distributed to the poor, by the U.S. government). Again, a disagreement between the two was brought to the pope's attention, and again the pope sided with Sheen. These two defeats humiliated Spellman and soured his relationship with Sheen.

5

LIFE IS WORTH LIVING

On television, as well as in the arts and sciences, he who appears before the public may well ask himself: "What powers hast thou that did not come to thee by gift? And if they came to thee by gift, why dost thou boast of them, as if there were no gift in question?"

—Fulton J. Sheen, *Life Is Worth Living*

Life Is Worth Living was a weekly half-hour program in which my uncle, speaking directly to the camera as though to the viewer, spoke on various moral and social issues such as hope, peace, loneliness, temptation, and mental illness, to name a few. He sometimes addressed political subjects (such as Communism) or spiritual ones (such as angels). His audience included people of all faiths. In a few short months, it was a bona fide hit.

During his show, people were glued to their sets. So much so, that in one particular case when a family was watching my uncle on TV, they didn't notice that they were being robbed! My uncle told the story on an episode. "It seems that within the last few weeks, the Murphy family was watching TV upstairs. A robber came in and took about three hundred dollars in cash and a couple of thousand dollars in jewels. The next day the robbers phoned and said, 'We found out that we were in the wrong house.

We are very sorry; we sure did have butterflies in our stomach when we saw Bishop Sheen on television.'" Then my uncle launched into a talk about conscience.

Just as I had gone to his radio show tapings, Jerry and I always went to the tapings of his TV show. It was fascinating to watch him. My uncle never wrote out his speeches. He just used notes—handwritten ones, mind you; he didn't type them. And he always made sure to have his ending ready. He would watch the clock, and then, at the proper moment, he would tack the conclusion he had prepared onto the end of his speech. He had it all timed. Since the show was live, he had to be really sure his talk didn't run over or under time. He was such a professional, you would think he had been on TV all his life—yet television was in its infancy at the time!

Life Is Worth Living is what he is most famous for, but I think it was when he became the national director of the Society for the Propagation of the Faith that my uncle really found his calling. My uncle was passionate about a lot of the things he did for God and the Church. He loved teaching at the university, writing books, and giving lectures. He loved administering the sacraments and hearing confessions, and he seemed to have an overall zest and enthusiasm for every aspect of his priesthood. Even so, I would have to say that out of all the things he did, the work he did for the missions was the greatest love of his life.

His love for the missions was different from his enthusiasm for anything else. For one thing, he would light up when he would talk about it. Whenever he came back from traveling on behalf of the missions—and he was dead tired—if you asked him how the trip went, his energy would return. He would begin to tell you all about the people he met and how they were suffering. He was very anxious to raise money for all of them.

I think he would have loved to have been an actual missionary himself. He felt that missionaries had a dedication to their vocation that went far beyond just being a priest. He saw all the hardships missionaries put up with and how they never complained. He was so impressed and moved by it all and wanted very much to be of help, too.

The Society—or the "Prop" as we called it—was the perfect platform for him to accomplish this. And he was the perfect person for the job. Who better than one of the world's most well-known and well-liked Catholics to be in charge of a worldwide fundraising effort for the missions? And when my uncle began to star on a weekly television show, he could appeal for help by directly reaching out to his viewing audience. He became a missionary extraordinaire—without having to leave the studio. He raised record-breaking funds for the missions worldwide. The pope was thrilled with him. Francis Cardinal Spellman, the archbishop of New York, was less so.

My uncle's visibility on *Life Is Worth Living* had also earned him other kinds of appreciation. He made the covers of both *TV Guide* and *Time* magazines. He also won an Emmy (beating out Lucille Ball, Milton Berle, and Edward R. Murrow) for Most Outstanding Television Personality. And by the end of his first season (the show would run for five years), my uncle had become the most prominent Catholic leader in the United States. This could not have made Cardinal Spellman happy. He was famously jealous of my uncle (much to my uncle's sadness) and would make my uncle's life more difficult later on.

House Hunting

Although he was more famous than ever, my uncle was still just my uncle to me, and both Jerry and I loved and missed him. We looked forward to his phone call every couple of months, when he would tell us to get a babysitter and come up to New York City for a few days. Jerry and I would book a hotel and then meet my uncle for dinner and a show. It was always great to catch up with him. When the three of us got together it seemed like old times.

When we went out to eat, one thing my uncle never did was drink wine with dinner. He never drank any kind of alcohol, period. He practiced temperance. I enjoyed a glass of wine with dinner, and he never objected to my (or anyone else's) drinking. He simply chose not to drink himself.

When my husband's job began decentralizing (he worked in the chief counsel's office at the Internal Revenue Service), we suddenly had a choice of places to live. My father thought we should move to Chicago to be closer to him; it was where he had wanted us to move when we were first married. But my uncle said, "New York! That's where you belong." I did have a lot of friends in New York and had, of course, grown up there, so I thought, "He's right. That's a great idea!" And New York it was.

Once again my uncle said, "I'll find you a house." And one evening he called and told me to get on the six o'clock train in the morning because he wanted to show me a house. "I don't need a big house," I warned him. "We can't afford a big house." And I told him what we could pay. "That's it," I said. "Don't get any crazy ideas."

And he didn't. My uncle was wise enough to know that even though Jerry's job was going to be in Manhattan, buying or renting a place in the city could be very expensive. He decided to look in Yonkers both for its affordability and because it had an easy commute to the city. There he found Burke Real Estate and thought, "That's a good Irish name." He walked in and told the agent plainly, "I need to find a house for my niece."

The agent showed him a good house in a nice location called Park Hill. "It's a very family-friendly place," he said, "and the Catholic school is within walking distance." My uncle was sold, but my husband and I didn't want to sign any papers until we saw it for ourselves. We should have just trusted my uncle, though, because the moment we saw it, we knew. And that was how we bought our first home in New York.

This Is ...

My uncle wrote many, many books in his lifetime (almost seventy). Many are considered spiritual classics now, like *Life of Christ*, *Three to Get Married*, *Lift Up Your Heart: A Guide to Spiritual Peace*, and so on. (I wish *Three to Get Married* was on the bestseller list right now! I think this world needs it.)

In the late fifties and early sixties, my uncle was contracted not so much to write as much as to "take part" in a series of four titles for Hawthorn Books: *This Is Rome*, *This Is the Mass*, *This Is the Holy Land*, and *These Are the Sacraments*. They were to be more like photo essays or coffee-table books featuring my uncle. The text of *This Is Rome* and *This Is the Holy Land* was actually written by the famous travel writer H. V. Morton. Henri Daniel-Rops, the French historian, wrote the text for *This Is the Mass*, and my uncle wrote the text for *These Are the Sacraments*. The photographs were taken by the legendary Armenian photographer Yousuf Karsh, best known for his black-and-white portraits of notable people.

The publisher sent my uncle, Morton, and Karsh to Rome and the Holy Land together to work on two of the books. My uncle invited me and my eldest son, Francis

Jerome, "Jerry", to go with them, and we traveled with the whole entourage.

When we got to Rome, we found that the publishers had put us up in a big, fancy hotel, which looked very inviting after our long flight. We were going out to dinner with the others, so I said to my son, "You'd better quick get in tub and get cleaned up." No sooner was he in the tub than there was a knock on the door. It was my uncle, who announced, "We're not staying here."

"But Jerry's in the tub," I said.

"Get him out, then, and pack your things. We're leaving."

I thought something must be wrong until my uncle explained that since we were going to be in Italy for a couple of weeks, he wanted to be in the little hotel where he usually stayed when visiting Rome. The management knew him, and he felt comfortable there, he said, but most of all, we would have more privacy. We would be able to come and go as we pleased, he explained, without attracting any notice. The fancy hotel, he added, was for people interested in being seen.

I asked about the others, and he said, "We'll meet up with them for dinner and such, but it will be much more fun if we can go where we wish and do as we please when we are not taking photographs for the book." So that's what we did. And he was so right.

We did a lot of walking around Rome, which could get tiring, especially for my son. He stayed in good humor for the most part. He could be a bit of a clown, too. For instance, the photographer, who lived in Ottawa, Canada, and whom everyone called simply "Karsh", had an artistic flamboyancy about him. He wore a big hat and cape. Very dramatic. One time when he was taking photographs, he laid the hat and cape on a nearby rock. Well, when my son saw them lying there he couldn't resist. They were like a costume! He put them on, and when Karsh saw him he didn't get mad—he took a picture. He always knew a good photographic opportunity when he saw it.

My favorite moment of the trip to Rome was meeting Pope John XXIII. My uncle was in awe of the popes (no matter which pope it was), and he had many audiences with them over the years. Whenever he was going to see a pope my uncle just seemed to get a different way about him. It obviously meant a great deal to him to meet with one—almost like getting an audience with God. That's how we all felt in those days.

After Rome, my uncle, my son, and I went to England and Belgium. In England we visited with some old friends of my uncle's. They had us for dinner at their typical London flat and told us that they made the fire in the fireplace bigger than usual as Americans seemed to mind the cold more.

After our tour of London, we went to Brussels. There we were met by representatives of King Baudouin and taken to his palace. My uncle's demeanor was the same at the palace as it had been in the London flat, as he treated everyone from all walks of life with the same amount of respect. I, of course, was in awe of seeing such a place. My son, however, was disappointed that the king greeted us wearing a blazer and slacks instead of a crown and robes.

Our trip to Israel for *This Is the Holy Land* happened a few years later. I was expecting a baby (my son Paul), so I couldn't go. When I told my uncle I was sorry but I would have to miss the trip, he turned to my husband and said, "Oh, Jerry, you could do it!" Jerry, who was sorry to have missed the last trip, realized that, yes, he could! He took along the two boys (Jerry again, as well as our other son, Fulton. They were ten and a half months apart and got along very well. My Irish twins, I called them). My poor husband had a harder time of it than I did, though. Looking after two boys in a foreign land tested him a bit. The toughest part for him was simply keeping them clean: making sure they changed and bathed regularly—and to find ways to launder their clothes.

You can see photographs of the two boys in *This Is the Holy Land* (as well as of Jerry in *This Is Rome*). When they got back, my husband was glad to report that our sons had adapted to travel in the Holy Land very well. I thought it helped that they were so comfortable around their great uncle. Traveling with him was like being anywhere else with him. They never hesitated to speak up when they thought it was important, just as they would at home, as when my uncle was first learning to play the organ. My sons thought he would play with a little too much enthusiasm, and they didn't shy away from asking him to tone it down.

My husband was afraid that the boys showed a little too much enthusiasm of their own when they posed for photographs for the book. That's because they didn't feel like it was "posing" so much as playing or playacting—which they liked a lot. They enjoyed interacting with the people and the scenery, and they had fun tracking down sheep near the Sea of Galilee. My uncle must have had fun, too, because his favorite photo of himself is one that Karsh took of him cradling a lamb by the Sea of Galilee. For his part, my husband was grateful that his sons were so engaged, but he spent a lot of time running after them, calling out, "Don't get dirty!" So it was both touching and funny that he brought home water from the River Jordan, which my uncle used to baptize Paul after he was born.

My husband did some posing, too—for the book *These Are the Sacraments*, where he is shown as a penitent receiving the Sacrament of Reconciliation. In the proofs was a photograph where all you could see of Jerry was his foot peeking out from underneath the curtain of the confessional. "I put my sole into it!" he quipped.

At least we didn't have to travel far to take the photographs for that book. We went to a church in Manhattan, where my daughter was photographed, too, as a First Communicant. One of my uncle's favorite chalices, made of jasper, was also included in the book. He willed it to Saint Patrick's Cathedral, where it remains to this day. The photographs were solemn, but we had fun making them, with lots of laughing and kidding around. Afterward we all went out to dinner together.

A Quiet Man for Others

What surprises some people about my uncle—especially since he was so well known for his public speaking and was friendly to strangers on the street—was that he was very introspective. He could be really hard on himself. He was always examining his conscience and quietly praying before the Blessed Sacrament. He kept a Holy Hour every day. Although he had this introverted tendency, he was never aloof. He would meet people at his broadcast— strangers—who would invite him over to dinner, and he would accept. There were so many families he took an interest in. They all loved him, and many named their sons Fulton. He baptized a lot of Fultons.

What is perhaps less surprising about my uncle is that he was very energetic. He had a stationary bicycle in his apartment, and sometimes while he was exercising he played phonograph records of Italian lessons. He loved to learn. He liked to be up on everything—not just religious subjects but social and political ones, too. He was very well rounded. I think that's why he could relate to so many people.

He was most drawn to simple, honest people, but he also enjoyed getting together with his fellow TV stars Milton Berle and Jackie Gleason (who were both popular at the same time that he was). Truth be told, they loved getting together with him. They considered him very funny. They were two classic comedic legends, but they laughed just as much at my uncle's stories as he did at theirs.

My uncle valued good humor as a virtue. His belly laugh was well known. He could get hysterical about some things. He always said, "If you don't have humor in your life, you're lost." That's why he enjoyed the company of my husband so much. Not that Jerry was a joke teller, but he could see the humor in situations and turn a word or a phrase around and make us laugh. He was also a very patient, peaceful type of person.

He could be very particular about things, such as hanging up a picture on the wall, and whenever my uncle needed to hang something he would call us up: "Jerry has to come and hang something for me." Jerry and I would get there, and Jerry would start measuring. This would make my uncle laugh. "You don't have to do that," he would say; "you just have to put a nail on the wall!" They had a lot of fun over that.

I have already mentioned my uncle's generosity, but here is another incident I must relate. Jerry and I had a burglary. Unlike the Murphy family in my uncle's story, none of us was home at the time—and we were grateful for that. But also unlike the Murphy family, we received no apology and didn't have anything returned. Truthfully, I was shaken up to know that someone had trespassed on my property and broken in to my own house. And I was heartbroken when I discovered that the thief or thieves had taken all of our sterling silver. My uncle heard about the robbery and called me the following week, inviting me to go down to the city and have dinner with him. I went to his apartment, intending to cook him dinner, when there, sitting on top of a table, I saw a small chest.

"That's for you to take home," my uncle said. "It's my silver. You're to take it."

His set was probably worth five times what mine was. I still use it. It's beautiful silver. But that was how my uncle was. He always tried to do things for others. If he saw you worried or upset, he tried to take your cares away.

A Shocking Loss

But there is some pain you just have to go through.

On July 4, 1960, my father had a heart attack while playing golf with my mother. He was rushed to the hospital. He recovered well enough for everyone to think his condition wasn't that serious. Even my mother felt comfortable enough to leave his bedside. It therefore came as a big shock to her—and to all of us—when he died later than night. He was only fifty-six.

My mother was inconsolable afterward. It was awful. I had just had a baby, but I was the one who had to call my uncle to tell him that his brother had died. I also had to call my uncle Tom.

I missed my father terribly. As we made his funeral arrangements, my younger sister told me that I was my father's favorite. I didn't contradict her. I actually thought she was right: I was his favorite. I didn't know why. Maybe because I was the first girl? I was in high school by the time my sister was born. She was only five years old when I got married. I had the advantage of knowing our father longer than she had. And for the blessing of those years I am truly thankful.

Fulton Sheen's Formula

There can be no doubt that Fulton Sheen was an exemplary priest. He is often now referred to as a "priest's priest", a model of how to live out the vocation with true joy. And by now we can see that he was constantly occupied with doing the work of God, whether it was by lecturing in a university, broadcasting on the radio, starring in a television show, traveling the world, or celebrating the sacraments. But how was he able to do it all? And (seemingly) indefatigably?

He had a simple but foolproof two-part formula. One that required his constant dedication, but that provided the fuel he needed to continue at the pace he felt called to take.

The Holy Hour

The first part of this formula was a daily practice: Eucharistic Adoration—praying before the Blessed Sacrament. On the day of his ordination, he resolved to pray in this way for one hour every day for the rest of his life. Although not always an easy resolution to maintain (for instance, he once prayed in an otherwise empty church and ended up getting locked inside and having to escape by crawling out of a window), he made sure to keep up the practice to the end of his days. One way he was able to do this was by making sure to have one room in his living quarters (no matter where he lived) converted into a chapel.

Over time he came to rely on the Holy Hour, craving its benefits and seeing his time spent before the Eucharist as akin to breathing with the help of an oxygen tank. He encouraged all he could to practice the Holy Hour as well, explaining that its purpose was to draw people closer to Christ: it was keeping company with Jesus when he suffered in the Garden of Gethsemane, anticipating his torturous death. According to the Scriptures, the night before he died the Lord could not find even one apostle to stay awake with him for one hour and offer him consolation. Sheen took it upon himself to offer that consolation to Jesus every day in this way for over sixty years.

In his autobiography he wanted his readers to know that he didn't want them to think that he was trying to boast of his personal holiness when telling them of his long-standing devotion. On the contrary, he was saying that without the daily Holy Hour he would not have the grace to even "keep step" with his fellow priests and their good works.

Devotion to Mary

The second part of his foolproof formula was a weekly practice: every Saturday at Mass, he offered up the Eucharist in honor of the Blessed Mother, asking her, in turn, to protect his priesthood through her prayers.

Sheen was famously devoted to Mary, the Mother of Jesus. He traced this devotion back to his own baptism, when his mother, Delia, not only had him baptized in a church named for her (Saint Mary's Catholic Church in El Paso, Illinois), but afterward laid her baby on our Lady's altar and consecrated him to her. This consecration created a sort of spiritual "birthmark" on his heart, and he felt drawn to Mary ever after, going so far as dedicating himself to her on his own after he received his First Holy Communion at the age of twelve. And as he grew up, he continually prayed for her assistance, intercession, and protection, and prayed the Litany to the Blessed Virgin every night.

Once he was an adult, his Marian devotion propelled him to visit shrines to Mary, especially the one in Lourdes, France (the site of miraculous apparitions of the Blessed Mother), and the one in Fatima, Portugal (where she was also said to have appeared). In his lifetime, he would visit Lourdes thirty times and Fatima ten. He would even later write a whole book about why one should be devoted to the Blessed Mother, called *The World's First Love: Mary, Mother of God*.

When he was ordained a bishop, Sheen chose a motto for his coat of arms to reflect his devotion: "Grant that I may come to Thee through Mary." He did this, he said, because he was never drawn to her without Christ. After all, "it was not the Church that made her important," he wrote once; "it was Christ himself." He compared their relationship to that of the sun and the moon. The immense and powerful light of the sun brings forth life upon the earth. The moon illumines the night, but not with its own light. Rather, it shines with the reflected light of the sun. Without the sun, the moon would be nothing. But thanks to the sun, the moon can illuminate our way at night, and we can its beauty—in much the same way that the Blessed Mother glows as she basks in the Look of Love the Lord casts upon her.

Since our Lady is also considered the special custodian of priests and their vocations as well as an advocate for their souls at their time of death, Sheen entrusted his vocation to her care. He hoped that when he was before the Judgment Seat of Christ Mary would have already put in a good word for him and that Jesus would say, "I heard My Mother speak of you."

6

THE ROCHESTER YEARS

Our Lord wants everything from us. He was the first "totalitarian" of the spirit: He asks that we hold nothing back from Him. He demands total love. "With thy whole mind, thy whole heart, thy whole spirit, and thy whole strength." Only those who have given their whole hearts to God can give Him their whole capital as well.

—Fulton J. Sheen, *From the Angel's Blackboard*

Losing my father had been very difficult. So years later, when I heard that my uncle was being made named bishop of the Diocese of Rochester and would have to move upstate, I was devastated. My uncle was like a second father to me. Having him sent away so suddenly made me feel like I was losing him, too. And although Rochester was still in New York, it was so far that we had to take a plane or an awfully long car ride to get there.

When my uncle broke the news of his impending move to me, I couldn't believe it. "Why in Heaven's name are you going up there?" I asked.

He said, "Well, you know, when I was ordained, I took a vow of obedience. So I have to go where they're sending me."

Everyone said that Cardinal Spellman was sending him to Rochester as a sort of banishment, as his terrific jealousy of my uncle was so well known. Some people even claimed that Cardinal Spellman had gone as far as to instruct other priests to refrain from inviting my uncle to speak at their churches. If that were true, it would certainly explain why my popular, educated, and famous uncle was not being invited to speak at events as he once had.

My uncle never spoke to me about his relationship with Cardinal Spellman. He didn't believe that any good could come from airing dirty laundry. Later, when the bishop's and the cardinal's remains both lay buried in the crypt under the Cathedral of Saint Patrick, I would smile at the thought that it appeared someone had taken pains to make sure there was a lot of marble between them.

When my uncle first arrived in Rochester, he stopped the outgoing (retiring) bishop from moving out of the lovely home he had enjoyed for years. "No, you stay there," he told him; "there's no need for that." And my uncle moved into an apartment over the bingo parlor. It was very nice. Large. And of course, he converted one of the rooms into a chapel, as usual.

Once he settled in, my uncle went out to get to know the people in his new diocese. He was pleased by the mix of ethnic groups he found there, since he was always interested in multiculturalism. But he was very distressed by the poverty that he encountered there as well. Rochester was the opposite of a booming town. Work was hard to find, and at the time there was also a noticeable lack of affordable housing. He saw an awful lot of poor people. I remember visiting my uncle there and seeing many Native American beggars standing on street corners. My uncle, as usual, gave them money, even though at the time that community was suffering from an alcoholism epidemic. Once again, I challenged his generosity. "What if they use it for drink?"

His answer? "I can't take that chance. Their children might be hungry."

He loved the poor, and there were a lot of poor. He went to homes all the time. He would say Mass in their living rooms. Other priests weren't doing that sort of thing, and certainly not bishops. I don't think the people of Rochester understood why their bishop was.

My uncle wanted to help the town of Rochester the best way he could, and he thought big. He couldn't help it. He was a big-city priest and a missions director. This gave him a global mindset. When he saw that the poor children of the city did not have access to adequate health care, he had this great idea to arrange for an ambulance that would go around, visiting the neighborhoods, providing checkups, and giving shots and things like that. But when he appealed to the hospital they didn't offer him any support for the idea, so he had to give it up.

He also famously wanted to close a barely used church and offer the real estate to the government so that they could use it to build affordable housing for the poor. Well, the people of Rochester practically stoned him. They literally threw rocks at his car and picketed against him. They revolted against the idea of his closing the church even though it was very poorly attended and their neighbors were in great need of housing. This violent reaction of the people came as a great shock to my uncle. It was a terrible, terrible time for him. I was upset for him, but he accepted it all as God's will. He just said, "That's all right."

He excused the people who reacted so violently. He said they didn't understand, that's all. He could excuse anyone. When people did something that wasn't exactly right, he could always find a reason for them. He really respected people. But the housing project idea ended up being another dream for Rochester that he had to abandon.

The funny thing is that the church was saved only to be eventually torn down years later (this time without a fuss) and replaced by affordable housing for seniors—which was then named after my uncle.

During his time in Rochester it seemed that his ideas and actions were always being thwarted. Apparently nobody wanted to change the way they were doing things, even if making a change would be for the better. So I definitely see my uncle's time there as a trial. Not that he ever said or expressed that. He suffered, but he didn't complain. He even would say it was "so nice" to be there. But I believe it was a real hardship for him. The one thing that I know that truly made him happy was the seminary, Saint Bernard's. My uncle was never really a parish priest. His only experience working in a parish was the year he was first ordained a priest and assigned to a parish in Peoria. His homilies were so instructive and well received that he was there only a year before his superiors felt that his talents were probably better suited for the world of academia. At Saint Bernard's in Rochester, my uncle was once again able to teach. In addition to teaching classes at the seminary, he also preached at retreats for priests, and for bishops, too.

My uncle brought professional speakers to the seminary because he thought it was very important for the seminarians to learn how to speak well and to become knowledgeable about their subject matter so that people would listen to them better. Future priests needed to learn how to present themselves well, especially since they would become "the face of the Church" to the public.

For a while I sent boxes of reels from his TV show and collections of his writings to the seminary every week to help them build the Sheen Archives. It pleased my uncle to know that priests and seminarians would be able to

have access to the materials he had used over the years and
hoped that they would find them as helpful as he had.

Like Mother, Like Son

My uncle managed to have fun in Rochester, too. Every
Saturday he would say Mass in a home—usually a very
poor home. During our visits to Rochester, we sometimes
went with him. We would process down the street, and
the people joining us for Mass would come out of their
homes to accompany us. He usually used a dining-room
table for an altar. If the family was Hispanic, we sang most
of the songs in Spanish, but he would give his homily in
English. The home would be overflowing with relatives
and neighbors who were happy to see the Church come
to them in this way.

One time a funny thing happened at one of these Masses
with my son Paul. My uncle gave all of my children their
First Communion, and he gave First Communion to all of
their classmates, too. The year my son Paul was preparing
for his First Communion, he attended a Mass with me
and the rest of his family in one of these private homes
in Rochester. At one point during the Mass, Paul rushed
up to the front. The rest of us stayed in the back. I wasn't
worried about being separated from him, because I knew
we would meet again afterward. When the Mass was over,
while we were waiting for him and my uncle to meet us,
one of my other sons approached me with a very serious
expression on his face.

"Do you know what Paul did?" he asked.

I felt immediate panic. "Oh no, what did he do?"

"He took Communion."

"He didn't."

"Yes, he did."

Paul wasn't due to receive Communion for six weeks! The minute Paul came out I asked him, "Did you take Communion?"

"Yes," he admitted, "the bishop gave it to me."

I asked him why he didn't tell the bishop (my uncle, of course) it wasn't his time yet. "Didn't you try to let him know?"

Paul just said, "But he gave it to me."

It reminded me of that time when my brothers and I took Communion when we weren't supposed to.

Once my uncle met up with us I told him what had happened. His reaction surprised me. "Isn't that wonderful? That's much better than being in a white suit!" He not only thought my son was ready, but he approved of the setting in which he received his First Communion.

Well, the parish didn't. When we got back and they heard that Paul had already received his First Communion, it was terrible. The parents of his fellow students had all wanted their children to receive from Bishop Fulton Sheen. Now that my uncle didn't need to be there for my son, he was not going to come, and there was an uproar. Poor Paul was made to attend his remaining classes and had to sit in the room when his classmates rehearsed for the First Communion ceremony that he was no longer going to be a part of.

My uncle also baptized my children. I would go to Mass every morning, and whenever the ladies at church noticed I was pregnant, they would ask, "When are you having the baby?" and "Would it be all right if we came to the baptism?" (They wanted to see Fulton Sheen, of course.) So I would reply with a shrug, "Sure. It's a church...." Then the word would get out.

On the day of the baptism, the church would be mobbed. My uncle thought it was grand, and he would give a talk. It was like a parish mission. Baptisms were held on Saturdays (rather than on Sundays), which made it easier to invite family and friends and have a brunch at home afterward. Seeing the crowds, my friends would ask, "These people aren't all coming back to your house for the party, are they?"

"No!" I assured them. (I had to draw the line somewhere.)

The Church and
the Modern World

Vatican II

Before he was assigned to Rochester, Fulton Sheen spent a good part of the early sixties participating in Vatican II. It surprises some admirers of Sheen that he was so involved in the Second Vatican Council, not to mention that he was such a great supporter of it, going so far as to call it one of the "greatest blessings the Lord bestowed" on his life. This is because Sheen is perceived as a conservative Catholic, and the Council is seen by some as more of a liberal event (or at least an event that resulted in liberal aftereffects). But (it may also surprise some) Sheen did not apply the label "conservative" to himself, nor did he see the Council as "liberal".

Opened on October 11, 1962, by Pope John XXII, the Second Vatican Council gathered bishops from everywhere in the world to examine matters of importance to "all of Christendom". It seemed to be the event that Sheen had been working toward his whole life. By then he had already published more than fifty books on various teachings of Christ and the Church and had traveled to nearly every continent and experienced the Church as expressed by peoples of all different cultures. At the Council, he was able to meet with bishops from all over the world, including some who have suffered under oppressive governments (e.g., through torture or imprisonment) for their faithful witness. He found it truly inspiring to be in their presence.

He participated in the four annual sessions of the Second Vatican Council (1962–1965), and in the first session was elected to the commission responsible for the Decree on the Missionary Activity of the Church *Ad Gentes*. (A theologian advisor on that same commission was Father Joseph Ratzinger, later, Pope Benedict XVI.) His most passionate interest during the proceedings was to promote the mission of the Church. He wrote, "Nowhere in the New Testament is any mention made of a distinction between the Church and its missionary activity. The Church in its very essence is missionary.... Priests are ordained for the mission of the Church.... The distinction between 'missionary' and 'non-missionary' priest is merely geographical. Every priest and every bishop is a missionary." He wanted the Church to remember the command to "go and tell all nations" and to make it a top priority. He had the privilege of being the last speaker on the subject of the missions, and his heartfelt speech (which went over the allotted time but he was not stopped or penalized for it) was well attended and met with applause at the end. His hard work paid off when the bishops voted in his favor, agreeing that "mission" was the essential work of the Church.

Ultimately he felt that the masterstroke of the Council was the Pastoral Constitution on the Church in the Modern World *Gaudium et Spes*, which stated that the dignity and freedom of the human person was inseparable from salvation. He felt that this document said nothing less than that the "new direction" the Church needed to take in order to continue spreading the faith was really the direction it had taken from her inception: to love God and neighbor as Jesus commanded.

But he saw clearly that there were two extreme points of view among the bishops regarding this idea, and in holding these views, they were continually separating the human person from salvation. He called these two groups the "conservatives" and the "worldlings", and he thought that they both refused to see that the two sides had to be combined and then balanced (to be in the world and not of it). The worldlings concentrated their efforts for social justice too much on an earthly level, while conservatives sought to enforce the faith in such a way that ignored the earthly level and failed to take into account the humanity, history, and culture of the people they wanted to convert. The stubbornness from both sides frustrated and saddened him.

He was also saddened by the general lack of appreciation and attention given to the Council documents. "Those who read the documents of Vatican Council II have no idea how much care and preparation went into every word they contained," he lamented. And most people (priests and laymen alike) did not read the actual documents but only read media interpretations of what they said. "It is quite wrong to think the Vatican Council brought on changes in the Church," wrote Sheen. "The Church does not live in a vacuum, but in the real world," which changes over time. It followed that the Church, being in the world, and being made up of people, was apt to change along with it. Christ himself was unchanging, as was his commandment that we love God, love ourselves, and love our neighbor. The challenge to present the unchanging Christ to a constantly changing world is one the Church has struggled with for over two thousand years and will continue to do so for years to come.

Dry Martyr

When a person is killed for espousing or refusing to deny his faith, that person is called a "martyr", which means "witness". Once a Catholic is considered truly martyred, he is almost guaranteed to be canonized a saint, provided a miracle can be attributed to his intercession.

Fulton thought there should be two categories for martyrs: "wet" and "dry". "Wet" being sort of shorthand for the spilling of one's blood. For literal, physical death. And "dry" for those who have endured long-suffering, such as being ill, imprisoned, or tortured. Not killed, but who have often suffered harder and longer than those who through their deaths were granted relief from more pain and suffering. And during the last decade of his life, through public humiliations and physical illness, Fulton would come to know some of the suffering of a dry martyr.

For years Fulton suffered under the hostility and simmering resentment of Cardinal Spellman, and when his archbishop finally sent him to Rochester under the guise of a promotion (after all, it was a step up to be put in charge of a diocese—albeit a crumbling one), it seemed obvious to many that Cardinal Spellman had sent Bishop Sheen into a sort of exile. Perhaps it was to keep him out of the spotlight or to punish Sheen for enjoying so many years in it. Still, true to form, and as he had in the past when assigned to serve in unglamorous positions in underdeveloped towns, Sheen humbly and obediently accepted the assignment, arriving in Rochester in 1966. He would last only three years there, and they would prove to be three of the most difficult years of his entire priesthood.

The sixties were a tumultuous decade in American history, and the idea of "revolution" seemed to define it. It applied to all areas of American culture: government, music, art, sex, race relations, social justice, and, of course, religion. Protests arose on a daily basis on the side of war or peace or social reform, and Rochester was as affected by the cultural turbulence as any other

American town during that era—or perhaps more so. It had been the site of riots just two years earlier due to a high unemployment rate (the result of businesses owned by Caucasians failing to hire or train African American workers), overcrowding (due to segregated and unfairly zoned housing), and tense relations between the police and the population.

Rochester was not the sort of assignment one would expect to be given to Bishop Sheen. To many he may have seemed a man from a different time, and those who did not know the sort of man he was perhaps imagined him ill-equipped to deal with the spirit of political and social unrest that seemed to permeate every avenue of the inner city there. But his sharp mind was constantly analyzing the state of the world, and he prayed constantly to be guided in his role as priest, as bishop, as shepherd.

He was also fresh from his experiences at the Second Vatican Council, and he was excited by the prospect of challenging evangelizing work—by the idea of bringing Christ to the people where they were at (or better yet, as he would say, not only to "bring Christ to them, but bring Christ out of them"). He wanted to let them know they were seen and heard by the Lord. So while he may not have chosen to be the bishop of Rochester, he believed that God called him there and that he would be able to get good work done in the Lord's name.

Sheen knew that as the bishop of Rochester he would be prayed for by name every day at every Mass said throughout the diocese! And he would need those prayers to sustain him. For it seemed, as Joan said, that every well-intentioned effort (such as the idea of affordable public housing) that her uncle put forth for the good of the diocese and its people was met with resistance, obstruction, and ultimately failure.

Joan Sheen (middle), her brother Bob, and her sister, Sue

Joan with Father Fulton Sheen, her uncle

Francis Cardinal Spellman (left), Bishop Fulton Sheen, and Joan

Walking with Governor Al Smith and his wife in New York City

Joan's graduation from St. Walburga's Academy, 1945

*Jerry Cunningham and
Joan Sheen*

*Wedding of Jerry and
Joan Cunningham,
October 29, 1949*

Father Fulton with one of his beloved dogs

Bishop Fulton Sheen with Jerry, Joan, Anne, and Paul Cunningham

Baptism of Joan's grandson, June 16, 1979

Archbishop Fulton Sheen's final resting place in Peoria, Illinois

Such as when he tried to get a page of "Catholic news" in the secular newspaper so that more people could read about the goings-on in the Church, not just locally, but globally. There was no internet at the time, and Catholic media outreach was truly minimal. But just when Sheen got close to cutting a deal with the secular press, he discovered that because of contractual issues, the idea had to be dropped.

In a precursor to the mall chapels of today, Sheen had the idea of buying a small storefront near a busy supermarket with a crowded parking lot and converting it into a chapel. There he hoped people would be able to stop in and pray before the Blessed Sacrament, receive the Sacrament of Reconciliation, or assist at Mass. This idea was also shot down as he was told that a storefront to suit his needs was impossible to find.

He gathered a council of construction workers, carpenters, and home-repair contractors and asked them to volunteer their weekends to teach black youths home repair while helping them fix their homes. He hoped that in turn, the young men would learn a trade and help their neighbors, thus enabling the community to build itself up both literally and figuratively. But this idea was seen as an infraction against union laborers and also rejected.

Worst of all, however, was the firestorm of criticism he received for his idea of the affordable housing project Joan mentioned. The idea met with opposition not only because it entailed tearing down a church (as Mass was poorly attended there and it was physically falling into disrepair, anyway) but because he had not consulted the priests of the diocese nor with its people of his idea. As a rule, communities do not like change, and like it even less when someone from "outside" comes and forces change upon them. Of course, Sheen had not seen it that way at all. He saw a need in the community and felt it the duty of the Church to fill it. He was working for them, not against them. He had thought his actions would be understood and had therefore not anticipated any opposition to the idea. Imagine the depth of his shock when people organized a protest rally against him!

Most disheartening for him, though, was when the petition against the housing idea crossed his desk, and he found that it was signed by a number of priests from his own diocese. The petition had the greatest effect: it stopped Sheen from going forward with the project, but it also hurt him very deeply to know that his "brothers" felt that he was someone who had done something that they needed to band together to fight against.

The priests and seminarians of Rochester had been particularly precious to Bishop Sheen. He felt that the most important domain of the bishop was a healthy, spiritual relationship with his brother priests and religious. He worked tirelessly at cultivating this. He saw to it that seminarians were being properly formed in the faith, and he personally led retreats for them and for his priests, too, considering that work to be "perhaps the most meaningful and gratifying experience" of his life. Such work, he said, forced the priest giving the retreat (in this case, him) to "review ... his own spiritual life", and so he would find himself to be almost as much "on" the retreat as the one giving it. When preaching at these retreats, he insisted on doing so in a church, before his beloved Blessed Sacrament, so that he could draw strength from that Real Presence of Christ (and invite laypeople from outside to come into the church and listen if they wished).

Sheen considered the bishop's power to ordain or "beget" other priests to be one of the best parts about being a bishop. Ordinations were his "supreme joy". However, he would not let his warmth and affection for the seminarians to deter him from refusing to ordain one if he felt that man to be unworthy of the vocation (and once was even thanked by the mother of a deacon he rejected who admitted that she agreed with his decision).

As a bishop, he knew that he was called to be a shepherd, and to imitate the Good Shepherd at that. Unfortunately, in Rochester it seemed as though every time he sought to lead his sheep to greener pastures he was prevented from doing so. By the time he reached the end of his third year in Rochester, he considered that his time there had been a failure. In 1969, as he was nearing retirement age, he went to Rome to tender his resignation to Pope Paul VI, who reluctantly accepted it and named him titular archbishop of Newport, Wales, an honorary position.

Sheen returned to New York, where he enjoyed ten years of retirement until his death in 1979. Until the end he led others to Christ, using even his own sufferings as a means to bring souls to God.

7

LOVE AND LOSS

Imagine the funeral service of a person who lived in sacramental and mystic union with Christ throughout his life. His body is dead beyond all doubt, but his soul lives, not only with natural immortality, which it possesses, but with the very life of God.

—Fulton J. Sheen, *From the Angel's Blackboard*

When the time came for my uncle to retire, he decided he wanted to live in New York City again. (Maybe that's one of the reasons why he called it "retreading" instead of "retiring". He would be sort of retracing his steps.) But before he could move back to the city, he needed to find an apartment.

That's when he called me up from Rochester. It was a Monday morning.

"What are you doing?" he asked.

"I'm making the beds, why?"

"Well, a car is going to come and pick you up at nine o'clock. You're going to have to find an apartment for me today."

"What?" I stopped smoothing out the sheet. "You know all these people in New York. You must know people in real estate, I'm sure. Why don't you just call one of them?"

"They would all just want to look for expensive apartments, and I can only afford so much," he said. Then he began to list his requirements. "I want a two-bedroom apartment so that I can convert one room into a chapel, as usual. I also want it to be on the East Side and with a view of the river."

I shook my head even though he couldn't see me. "You've got to give me more time!"

"I've cancelled all my appointments for today so that I can fly down to the city. Now, once you find the apartment, pick Jerry up in the car and have him take a look at the lease, since he's a lawyer. Then come and pick me up from the airport and I will sign it."

"You've got to be kidding me."

"I know I can rely on you, Joan. You've always done everything I asked."

I wondered how I was going to manage to snag an affordable apartment in the city in one day. "Can I at least tell people it's for you?"

"Yes. But remember I can only afford so much."

After I hung up with him, I called Jerry and told him the story. "Make sure you're available."

Jerry also couldn't believe it. "He doesn't really think you're going to find an apartment today. He's teasing you, Joan. But go, and have a look around," he advised. "Maybe you'll find a couple worth his coming down to have a look."

Soon I found myself sitting in the back of the car my uncle had sent for me, armed with only the *New York Times* real-estate section and the bishop's faith in me to get the job done.

The driver was an old friend of my uncle's, an Italian fellow named Mario who used to drive my uncle around the city years before. He kept saying to me, "Joan, this is crazy," as he drove me up and down the East Side, stopping at any building with an apartment that had been advertised in the paper and sounded like even a remote possibility.

When it got to be near one o'clock, I realized that the bishop was going to be arriving at the airport soon. I told Mario to take me over to York Avenue, because that's by the river. We drove for a few blocks around the seventies when I saw a white apartment building that had a river view on one side. The address was not listed in the paper as having an apartment for rent, and there was no sign outside advertising an apartment. But I decided to take my chances. "Pull over," I said to Mario. "I'm going in there."

When I met the building manager I said, "I'm looking for an apartment for my uncle Bishop Fulton Sheen. He needs a two-bedroom with a river view, but he can only pay so much ..."

The manager looked at me in surprise. "This is unbelievable! A couple just called up today. They had signed a lease, and they wanted to break it because they're now interested in buying another place." He smiled at me. "It's got a river view, it's got two bedrooms, and I think you'll find it fits within his budget."

The apartment was move-in ready. And later that day when my uncle walked through its front door, he loved the place at first sight. By six o'clock that evening he had signed the lease.

And that's how I got my uncle his apartment. They say one good turn deserves another: he got me my first home in New York, and I got him his last one. He lived there until he was eighty-four, almost ten years.

The Happy Giver

And they were happy years for the most part. He really loved it there. He got to know all the people in the building, and they were all very nice. He loved them, and they loved him. When he walked down the street, people would stop to talk and laugh with him. He would give them little crosses or religious medals, or money—whatever he had in his pocket that he thought they could use or might brighten their day. He got to know all the shopkeepers in the neighborhood. And when I would visit him with the kids, he would take them to the bakery and buy them sweets just as he had done with me when I was little.

The bishop was always very, very good to me and my children. Practically everything in my house is from him. People were always leaving him things in their wills and estates—which he appreciated—but which he would always give away to friends or to charity. I had a big house before the one I live in presently, and it was chock-full of furniture he had given me. Now all my children have it.

He had beautiful taste, too. His favorite color scheme to decorate in was red and gold. I think it gave his home a "churchy" look. (Speaking of "churchy", I still have a kneeler he once gave me before he moved to Rochester. It's wooden and rather plain since there's no padding on the kneeling part. Attached to it are a little statue of our Lady and a medallion. I think it's French-made. I saw him pray on it many times before he gave it to me.)

I think the thing he gave me that I cherish most is a beautiful portrait of himself as a young priest. It's an oil painting by Gerald Brockhurst and is something very, very dear to my heart. He gave it to me before he moved to Rochester. His eyes seem to follow you around, and sometimes people feel odd having a drink with him watching!

When my uncle died, he left everything he had to the Church, but he had also written a letter to Bishop O'Meara saying there were a couple of things he wanted me to have if he was allowed to leave them to me. My uncle then listed a number of items (such as a small dining table, a marble table, and a large lamp) that we had bought together while shopping for things for his new apartment.

Before he had moved in, my uncle and I went shopping every week for furniture and other things he needed to make the apartment ready for his official arrival. When we saw the dinette set we knew it would fit perfectly in his apartment since it had only an eat-in kitchen and no formal dining room.

When other people found out my uncle was moving back to Manhattan, they offered to help. One man volunteered to design and furnish the chapel. He was a set designer, and he did a lovely job. He took a small bedroom and had it draped from top to bottom in all shades of blue in honor of our Lady. Even the carpeting was blue. My uncle, whose favorite poem-prayer about Mary was "Lovely Lady Dressed in Blue", thought it was just great.

That chapel was where he baptized my daughter's firstborn child. At the time my uncle was very sick, but he wanted to baptize the baby anyway. The baptism could not be the big public affair that my own children's baptisms had been, and was instead a private, family affair, conducted in the little, cozy blue chapel inside my uncle's New York City apartment.

The baby was named John Paul. My daughter, Anne, and her husband weren't actually thinking of the pope at that time, John Paul II, when they chose their son's name, but my uncle was thrilled about it. He was, in fact, in awe of John Paul II. After he met him, he said, he came away feeling like he had really met the head of the Church.

Heartaches

I mentioned my uncle being very sick. He was suffering from heart trouble. One very sad thing I can never forget:

when he was first diagnosed, his doctor told him he must give up tennis. He loved tennis. It was his favorite sport. I had watched him play the game with much enthusiasm ever since I was a young girl. He even played it weekly when he could. It was his only passion in life that wasn't church-related.

But the doctors told him the "stop and go" wasn't good for him. When he called to tell me, he sounded very, very sad. He belonged to a tennis club where he used to play against a regular tennis partner. "Now ... I've got to clean out my locker," he said. Jerry and I went with him. He took out his terry-cloth robe and told me to give it to one of my boys. And it went on like that. It was the saddest thing to see—like watching a child giving up his toys, one by one. Jerry and I ended up taking all these things home.

The next day he decided to learn to play the organ.

Years later, when he was retired and living in his Manhattan apartment, his heart trouble got bad enough to warrant surgery. Unfortunately, some complications resulted from his first operation and he ended up needing another. He lost a lot of blood and became so weak he could hardly so much as lift his head. When word got out, though, there were firemen and policemen lining up to donate blood for him!

Despite all that, he still managed to carry out many priestly duties.

In his autobiography he wrote: "The second year after my open-heart surgery ... I was confined to my bed again for many months. During that time I instructed four converts and validated two marriages. The horizontal apostolate may sometimes be just as effective as the vertical."

Due to his long hospitalization, my uncle was no longer able to head the Propagation of the Faith, so his great friend Bishop O'Meara took over. He would visit my uncle at the hospital and helped my uncle say Mass in his bed.

In the hospital my uncle asked that his face be shaved twice a day. He was always such a proper person, and he wanted to be sure to represent the Church well in case someone came to visit him. That's why it so surprised me when I saw him wearing a robe and walking down the hospital corridors. I never, ever dreamt I would see him looking like that in public. But he was a humble man, and even when he was very ill, if he could walk, he would stop in other rooms to visit the other patients. He would joke with them and comfort them and advise them to take advantage of their suffering and offer it up to God. Priests often visit the sick in this way, but I think his visits had more power because he was famous and because he was sick and suffering just as they were. Most of all, because he had real faith in what he was saying. He may have made a few converts on his "rounds"!

My uncle once spoke about Maxwell Jones, a British psychiatrist who introduced a program called community care into a hospital. My uncle explained, "The project was that each person should have contact with those either in the same room or, if he was ambulatory, on the same floor. He was to consider himself part of the healing community. No one was to talk about his illness, but to bring solace to others.... Patients recovered quickly because they were loved." I think this is basically what my uncle was trying to do during his hospital stay, and I believe it helped to heal him as well as others.

The archbishop of New York at the time was Terrence Cardinal Cooke, and he was a very good friend of my uncle. Naturally, he also went to see him in the hospital. He never made any big to-do about it; he would just arrive—without announcing it ahead of time or with any fanfare.

When my uncle's hospital stay dragged on, I began to fret about the bills, but I was told not to worry, that the cardinal said he would take care of everything. He did, but it also ended up that none of the doctors really ever charged for their services to my uncle, either.

People from all over sent my uncle presents during his hospital stay, and my uncle always shared his "loot" with his fellow patients. I remember his neighborhood pastry shop (where everyone knew and loved him) sending him a basket of cookies. Sadly, my uncle wasn't allowed sweets while he was recovering, so he gave them out to other patients and staff.

And the gifts kept coming, even when he was finally back home. The doormen loved it whenever packages were delivered to my uncle. They would take them up to him and he would say, "Let me peek in the box and see the card," and then, "Take them home to your children."

Death of a Saint

The last I saw him was on a Friday in December. He asked me and my husband to come down to his apartment. "My books are just a mess," he told us and asked for our help to put them in order.

Books were very important to my uncle, and he did a lot of reading during his convalescence in the hospital. Sometimes wanting certain books to read in particular, he would ask his friends to go over to his apartment and get them. They would, but over time, the books on his shelves fell into disarray.

"They're all jumbled up," he said, "and before I arrange my bookshelves again, I would like to get rid of some of them, send some up to Rochester, and give some away." It was too big a project for an eighty-four-year-old man with heart disease so severe that even bending over might be too strenuous for him.

Jerry and I were in our fifties and pretty healthy. Once we arrived, my uncle sat on a chair and directed us as we separated his books into stacks. Then I cooked him his favorite weekly meal: a tiny hamburger, little canned peas, and Kadota figs for dessert.

When we went home that evening, I said to Jerry, "He's never seemed so well. At last he seems like he's back to himself."

Two days later he was dead.

I was shocked that Sunday when Monsignor O'Mara called to tell me. The people who found my uncle's body called Cardinal Cooke right away, and he went up to the apartment.

The cardinal was very kind to us, wanting to accommodate us as much as possible while making the arrangements for my uncle's funeral. Someone from his office called to tell us, "The cardinal would like Bishop Sheen to be buried in the crypt under the altar at Saint Patrick Cathedral." I said I thought that it would be a wonderful honor.

Cardinal Cooke even volunteered to have a luncheon for the family at his residence, but I declined. There were so many people from out of town to accommodate. Besides, my house was big enough to hold them all, and all our neighbors had gotten together and said they would take care of the rest of the details.

My uncle's body was laid out at the Frank E. Campbell Funeral Home and then brought down in a funeral procession to Saint Patrick's Cathedral. There they received the body and laid him out so that the public could view him. His coffin was placed in the main aisle. Jerry and I were there the whole time as people came by to pay their respects. Most people prayed when they reached the body. Some wept. Others even touched him. It was an emotional experience. Every day was hard, really. I also heard from relatives—many I hadn't heard from in years, others I didn't even know—who called me. They all wanted to have a seat at the funeral.

He was laid out for days, and they had different Masses for him each night. One night, the Propagation of the Faith had the Mass; Rochester had theirs another night. It seemed as though the Masses would go on forever.

Bishop Edward T. O'Meara gave a beautiful eulogy. He said, "A voice is silent in the midst of the Church and in our land. The like of which will not be heard again in our day. The vocation of Fulton Sheen is consummated: he has responded with one final 'yes' to the call of God. A 'yes' so final that human frailty and infirmity can never reverse it."

The bishop had been appointed the archbishop of Indianapolis and moved there soon after the funeral.

The funeral Mass was packed. Billy Graham was there. He loved my uncle. Leaders of other religious faiths also attended. An influential rabbi from the synagogue on Fifth Avenue came. So did Reverend Robert Schuller, the Protestant televangelist who preached from the famous Crystal Cathedral in California. (Revered Schuller's television ministry was inspired by the bishop's. The reverend greatly admired my uncle and invited him to talk at the cathedral a few times. Later he had a bronze statue of my uncle made and installed at the cathedral. Funnily enough, the Crystal Cathedral was recently purchased by the Diocese of Orange. It is now Christ Cathedral, a Catholic Church.) I thought it was a lovely tribute to my uncle to have Jewish and Protestant leaders photographed at his funeral. It showed just how much he had influenced people—not only Catholics. Of course, the TV show had a lot to do with this. It appealed to everybody. And so, in the same way, his death also seemed to touch everyone.

I was, of course, terribly sad, but as I grieved, I couldn't help but remember the one thing my uncle had always taught me: God is good. "Always appreciate all that God does for you," he said, "be they small things or big things. And always say, 'God is good.' Whether wonderful things happen, or difficulty arises, or sadness comes: God is good." So even though I was already missing my uncle very much, I could not fail to appreciate the reason why I was even grieving. It was because God had been so good as to give me an exceptionally kind and saintly uncle, and to allow him to help raise me in such a special way. Yes, God is good, I thought. So very good.

Suffering

As Joan described in the previous chapter, the bishop began to suffer from serious heart trouble in the mid-to-late 1970s, which required two open-heart surgeries and long stays in the hospital. He did, however, believe that the sufferings he endured (he almost died on three separate occasions) were not only gifts to him from God—but given to him through his beloved Lady, the Blessed Mother. Why through her particularly? He could not help but notice that he either needed surgery or would fall severely ill on her feast days! His first surgery was on the Feast of Our Lady of Mount Carmel (July 16), the second on the Feast of the Assumption of Mary (August 15), and he came down with a serious kidney infection on September 8 (when her birthday is observed), which gave him "tortures" for weeks.

Suffering has spiritual value, and when enduring illness or hardships, Catholics are often told to "offer it up." But what does that mean, exactly? On an episode of *Life Is Worth Living*, Sheen explained that the phrase first refers to expiation—a kind of deposit into our "Eternity Account" to pay against the debts that we have each accrued by our sinfulness so that "our ledger on the last day will not find us in the red." Secondly, it refers to reparation. That is, instead of our using our pain and suffering to serve only ourselves in expiation, we could use it on behalf of others, for their redemption. There are such things as blood transfusions, he said. Why not use your suffering to give a donation of grace to another person who might be greatly in need of it and with no one else to pray or sacrifice for them? It was a "great tragedy", he said, that "most people who suffer have no one to love", because love had to be the motive for both expiation and reparation. Love of God and love of neighbor.

He gave an example of reparation in his autobiography where he recounts one of the times his physical suffering was so severe (he even described the pain as "agony") that he felt himself hovering close to death. At that same time, he heard a nurse announce that the patient in the next bed was also on the brink of death. Armed with this knowledge, but sapped of strength, Sheen knew what he was being called to do. He offered up his sufferings for the salvation of his neighbor's soul, and through the greatest of effort and the tiniest of movements of one finger, made the sign of the cross, granting him conditional absolution. The gentleman died immediately after the blessing, in a state of grace.

Fulton was not afraid of death. He wrote, "Our Lord told us ... we were not to fear dying, nor to fear being 'called on the carpet' for our faith, nor to fear economic insecurity, nor to fear the future." He had been taught since his sophomore year in high school to pray to Saint Joseph for the grace of a happy death, and it remained a daily practice for the rest of his life to say three Hail Marys for that intention. While he did so, he would ask the Blessed Mother to intercede so that he could die on one of her feast days, preferably on a Saturday, the day of the week that is also dedicated to her. When he told this to Malcolm Muggeridge, the famous journalist and convert corrected him, saying that Sheen should be ready to die on any day of the Lord's choosing. In his autobiography Sheen admitted that in the end it didn't matter when he died, that he would trust our Lady to cooperate with the will of God so that his death would be the most direct route to God. The day he died was very close to his wishes: Sunday, December 9, 1979, the day after the Feast of the Immaculate Conception.

Sheen wrote in his book *Peace of Soul*:

> The acceptance of death is ... a manifestation of our Love of God, [because] at the moment of death, when the soul leaves the body, we shall be judged not by the earthly advantages that we had—beauty or talent, or the wealth that accompanied the body, or the social advantages— but only by the degree to which we responded in Divine Love.... When a soul has proved that it loved God above all things ... it is prepared to stand before Love."

Sheen died at home, collapsing just outside his private chapel, probably after having finished his Holy Hour. Although his body was found on the floor, we imagine and pray that his soul found itself standing before God, just as he described above, immersed in that Divine Love that Sheen so eloquently described. Many pray that he will be declared a saint soon.

Being an intelligent and generous priest isn't enough for the Church to declare a man a saint. So why is it that people believe Fulton Sheen should be canonized? Let us pause for a moment to recall the spiritual gifts that shone through holy men and women of the past that helped them to be recognized as saints.

The gift of preaching was apparent in Saint Paul and Saint Anthony of Padua. They were known to be elo-quent speakers that moved scores of people to convert to Christianity. The inspired writings of Saint Thomas Aqui-nas, Saint Teresa of Avila, and Saint Thérèse of Lisieux have helped countless numbers to come to know the Lord.

So much so that they were all later accorded the very special title of "Doctor of the Church", given to those considered to be outstanding contributors to Church doctrine or theology.

Then there are those "Defenders of the Faith", such as Saint Ignatius of Loyola, Saint Francis de Sales, and Saint Vincent de Paul, unafraid to speak up on behalf of God, even before great opposition. And let's not forget the great evangelizers, those who spread the Gospel throughout the world, such as Saint Francis of Assisi, Saint Augustine, and Saint Patrick. Or those known for the gift of counsel like Saint Catherine of Siena.

The truth is, Fulton J. Sheen had all these gifts in common with the great saints.

8

LEGACY

Turning around the statement of the savior, Our Blessed Lord was saying that no old people will ever enter the Kingdom of Heaven—old in the sense of being wise in their own conceits. I shall look for you in the nurseries of Heaven.

—Fulton Sheen, *From the Angel's Blackboard*

I pray for my uncle's intercession. Nothing formal. I just talk to him. Sometimes I come in through my living room, catch sight of his painted portrait there, and say, "Hi." He's still very much alive to me. Sometimes I come across something he gave me, like a piece of jewelry, and I feel as though he is still around.

And just recently something hit me very strongly. I was remembering how when I was a child I would sometimes complain to him about things (maybe about the nuns or something that happened at school) and he would just listen. He never chided me or insulted me when I complained. He didn't say I was being stupid or childish. But he always tried to help me see the better part of a situation. He would tell me that when something really bothered me or if something bad seemed to be happening to me, to try to think of one good thing that could come out of it.

I remembered this recently because I not long ago fell flat on my face—on cement. I had a black eye, and I had to have stitches on my nose—my whole face was a mess. Oh, I got such sympathy, it was wonderful. And I thought to myself, "God is good." I didn't break a hip. This perspective is what my uncle taught me.

Protection of a Saint

All my friends tease me about how my uncle protects me. It's funny, because as I previously mentioned, I have a place down at the beach, and when Hurricane Sandy came, all the lights went out in the neighborhood—except at our place. All the other houses in the neighborhood basically lost their first floor, yet our house was not touched. People (even those who don't go to church a lot) say, "That's because of your uncle" or "The bishop saved your house." Of course I think there's some truth to it since I really believe that he does watch over me.

But when things do go wrong in my life—such as when I suffer a loss—I remember my uncle telling me to accept such things as God's will. He came up to the house when one of my sons died while still a young man, and he said, "Joan, God never gives you a cross without enough strength to bear it."

Remembering his words has really helped me through the more difficult times of my life. Like when my husband, Jerry, died.

Some years ago, Jerry and I were planning on going to Florida. I had a trustee meeting at the hospital that morning, and when I was there I told the doctor, "Oh, Jerry's coming over to see you tomorrow. He said a funny thing to me. He was in a hurry to get dressed or something and he said, 'Maybe you're going to have to help me button my shirt. I'm having trouble with my fingers.'"

The doctor looked up from his computer and asked, "He was having trouble breathing a while back, wasn't he? Didn't you bring him to the emergency room?"

And I said, "Yes. I've had to take him to the hospital a couple of times for that."

Jerry went to see a neurologist who diagnosed him with ALS—amyotrophic lateral sclerosis (better known as Lou Gehrig's Disease). When we got the news, I called my brother Jack, who's a doctor, and had him take a look at Jerry. But he only agreed with the neurologist's diagnosis.

"Joan," he said, "I hate to tell you this, but he has the worst kind. He has about eighteen months to live." And that's exactly how long Jerry lived after being diagnosed.

His breathing had been affected right away—which is normally what happens at the end. That's why he didn't last very long. And while his hands weren't good, he could walk up and down the steps. (My first thought when I heard the news was "How is he going to climb the stairs?" But he managed.)

Jerry accepted his illness just as my uncle would have advised him to. My husband was a man of deep faith. Even when it was no longer easy to kneel, he still knelt down every morning to say his prayers. And he went to work every day until the end.

My uncle understood suffering. He wrote a lot about it, too. One idea he returned to a few times was that the human capacity for pain is greater than the capacity for pleasure. He wrote, "Suffering reaches the point where we feel we can endure it no longer, and yet it increases and we endure it. But pleasures very quickly reach a peak and then begin a decline.... Our capacity for pain is greater because the Good Lord intended that all pain should be exhausted in this world. The Divine Plan is to have real joys in the next life."

This hope brings me comfort.

Jerry would come home in the afternoon and take a rest, because he had to, but all he really wanted to do was go, go, go. I helped him with his work as much as I could. I even helped with an audit by the IRS.

Many of his clients were retired school teachers from Yonkers. He was so handsome and humble, and a very sweet man, and these elderly women trusted him and recommended him to each other. He would say to them, "You paid all of these hospital bills. Now did you submit these to get reimbursed?" Many of them, overwhelmed by the idea of chasing after insurance claims, would say, "Oh, I don't think it's worth doing all that."

And he would reply, "Don't worry, my wife can do it for you." Then he would bring all this paperwork home, and I would submit the insurance claims for these elderly women who didn't know how to do it. This gave me an opportunity to do what my uncle had taught me: "Be generous with your time for others."

When Jerry died they all came to his funeral. My children asked, "Who are all these weeping people?" The schoolteachers wailed, "We'll never find an honest lawyer again!"

Jerry was honest. He had such a reputation for honesty, in fact, that he ended up doing tax work for Richard Nixon. Nixon had confided in a friend of ours that he was looking for a tax lawyer who would be completely above board because he didn't want any more problems with the law. When our friend heard this, he said to Nixon, "I know just the person (meaning Jerry)."

Our friend asked Jerry to meet with Nixon in New York, but he was reluctant. "I really don't feel like getting involved in something like this," he said.

"You're doing him a favor," I said (looking on the bright side, just as my uncle taught me.)

On the day of the meeting, Jerry threw out his back. "This means I shouldn't go," he said, almost relieved. "I should call and cancel." But his friend wouldn't let him off the hook, even if he was hunched over. The moment Nixon saw Jerry come through the door he scrambled to get him a chair. He was very considerate and attentive to Jerry, and very appreciative of all the work Jerry did for him. When Jerry died, Nixon wrote me a letter saying, "Even when he told me I had to pay more taxes I couldn't say a word!"

Frequently I dream of Jerry and my uncle. These dreams are usually about ordinary types of situations. I hope they are together again, having a chuckle over me trying to write a book! Actually, sometimes I think that's why I've remained in such good health all these years: to help to perpetuate my uncle's memory.

Saint Fulton

When Pope Benedict XVI pronounced Fulton Sheen "Venerable" in 2012, it was wonderful to know that the Church would be perpetuating his memory, too. It was so exciting because it seemed as if my uncle was well on track to being canonized a saint. But what happened instead was the process slowed down ... down ... down ... until it came to a screeching halt. The obstacle blocking the tracks? My uncle's body.

You see, a "turf war" of sorts broke out between the dioceses of Peoria and New York as to which had the greater right to his remains. Even though his body already lay housed in a place of honor in the crypt beneath the altar of Saint Patrick's Cathedral, Peoria challenged these arrangements.

My uncle was *from* Peoria, they pointed out, where there was already a museum set up in his honor, which was becoming a popular destination site for pilgrims and fans. If he was canonized and the body of their native son and homegrown saint returned to them, it would no doubt be a boost to the tourism and the economy there.

New York's argument was just as valid. My uncle had spent many more years living there than he ever had in Peoria. He had executed much of his life's work of preaching and teaching there, and, of course, he had died there. And with remains already there—and in a place of honor, no less—why should his final resting place be disturbed? New York was both a city and a state that he had adopted in his heart, and it had taken him in as one of their own. But did New York—or Saint Patrick's Cathedral—need more tourists? Did their economy need a boost? Could my uncle's remains even be venerated properly in that tiny, cramped, rarely opened crypt?

What would Fulton Sheen have wanted? We asked each other. The truth was, he had told us what he wanted in his will, where he asked to be buried in New York— *but* in a cemetery where he had already purchased a plot. He hadn't expected the honor of being buried in the crypt. But again, this just meant that neither Peoria nor Saint Patrick's Cathedral could claim that he had specifically requested to be buried at either location.

So the battle raged on, and as it did, I began to worry that I would not live to see my uncle canonized. It seemed such a shame, too, that something as beautiful as being declared a saint of the Church was being hampered by politics and bad blood between dioceses. I knew that my uncle would never have wanted for such a situation to arise between them—let alone for he himself to somehow be at the root cause of the situation. But something I also knew was that despite everything, all the parties involved wanted to see Fulton Sheen declared a saint. In fact, I believed that my uncle himself would want the canonization process to proceed. Not because the extra title of "saint" would give him even greater glory after his death. No! My uncle would want to be canonized because it would give him more power to serve Christ and the Church as not only an inspiration, but also an intercessor at the disposal of the faithful. So, I was torn as to what I should do, as his closest living relative. After much thought and prayer, I remembered how humble my uncle could be, and I came to believe that, in truth, he would not really care where his remains were kept—as long as his eternal soul got to rest with God.

I made my decision and petitioned to have his body moved from the Cathedral of Saint Patrick in New York to the Cathedral of Saint Mary in Peoria. This surprised some until I pointed out that it was the Peoria diocese—not New York—that (back in 2002) had opened the cause for my uncle's canonization in the first place. (In fact at that time, New York *passed*, deciding not to pursue it.) So, it seemed to me that having my uncle's remains transferred there would be the best way to acknowledge and even reward Peoria for all the work they had put into his cause. It was also keeping in the spirit of my uncle, who always gave of himself.

After the final resting place of Fulton Sheen was finally resolved, his remains were moved to Saint Mary's Cathedral in June 2019. A month later, Pope Francis approved the miracle that paved the way for his beatification, and "Venerable Fulton Sheen" became "Blessed Fulton Sheen". At last his canonization was back on track.

The miracle was very touching. In 2010, the parents of a stillborn son prayed to Fulton Sheen for his recovery. After one hour (sixty-one minutes actually) without a pulse, the baby's heart began beating. The child was named James Fulton Engstrom and lives today without any health complications. The team of experts who evaluated the case said there was no medical explanation for it.

In addition to miracles, the Church requires proof of character before declaring a person a saint. I was so happy when the bishops evaluating my uncle's life said he was a man of "heroic virtue", although I don't think my uncle would like to be remembered as a "holy man". He didn't like to be seen in that way. I think he preferred to be seen as a servant of the Church, as its promoter or ambassador, even. Not as a "famous" person or a "pious" person, but as someone who lived and spread the Gospel.

I also don't think he would want to be known as the patron of television. There is a patron of television already, anyhow—Saint Clare of Assisi. I think he would want to be known for something earthier—something more relative to the real lives of people. Maybe something to do with the missions since they were such a big part of his life.

One very distinctive characteristic of his was his faithfulness to his Holy Hour. As much as he enjoyed preaching and teaching, in his heart of hearts what he liked best was to sit in the chapel and concentrate on the good Lord. He would write his books and letters in the chapel, sitting before the Eucharist. And the chapel was also the first place he went when things were overwhelming—for example, if he felt that he didn't give a good-enough talk or if he felt he failed to turn someone around. He would just go and sit with the Lord, just the two of them. It gave him comfort. That's why he had a chapel built in all of his homes.

Still at Work Today

Fulton Sheen would make a good saint for our times because he is still so relevant today. Many of his books are still in print and readily available. They still have the power to change hearts and lives. Same goes for episodes of *Life Is Worth Living*, which play sometimes on EWTN and can also be found on YouTube. He still has wide appeal.

He wrote and spoke on topics that are still current issues, like abortion and marriage. These are subjects that are in the headlines practically every day. And he spoke on these things in an intelligent way. He was nonthreatening and, even more importantly, nonjudgmental. He never "preached" to me, but I always got the message. He was a very kind person.

When people hear I am related to him, it means so much to them, and they are moved to tell me stories of how he has helped them. People have told me about how they turned on the TV to *Life Is Worth Living* and heard him say just what they needed to hear. Others have told me of how they picked up one of his books, read his explanation of something, and found it to be just what they needed to understand. Still others have told me that they have prayed directly for his intercession and have received his assistance in their time of need. And interestingly, I have found that often people who were helped by my uncle in these ways have connected to other people who were also helped by him. So, just as he did in life, my uncle is still bringing people together.

I would like to close this book with a prayer by Saint Francis de Sales. I came across it the other day and felt that it best expressed the way my uncle advised me to live my life and faith, trusting always in God.

Be at Peace
Do not look forward in fear to the changes of life;
rather look to them with full hope as they arise.
God, whose very own you are,
will deliver you from out of them.
He has kept you hitherto,
and He will lead you safely through all things;
and when you cannot stand it,
God will bury you in his arms.

Do not fear what may happen tomorrow;
the same everlasting Father who cares for you today
will take care of you then and every day.
He will either shield you from suffering,
or will give you unfailing strength to bear it.
Be at peace,
and put aside all anxious thoughts and imagination.

To which I add: God love you.

SOURCES

The following are the sources for the quotations from the published works by Fulton J. Sheen.

From the Angel's Blackboard: The Best of Fulton J. Sheen. 1st ed. Liguori, Mo.: Triumph Books, 1995.

Life of Christ. New York: Maco Magazine, 1954. Reprint, San Francisco: Ignatius Press, 2018.

Life Is Worth Living. New York: McGraw-Hill, 1953 and 1954. Reprint, San Francisco: Ignatius Press, 1999.

Lift Up Your Heart: A Guide to Spiritual Peace. Liguori, Mo.: Triumph Books, 1997. Originally published as *Lift Up Your Heart.* New York: McGraw Hill, 1950.

Peace of Soul. New York: Liguori, Mo.: Triumph Books, 1949. Originally published: New York: McGraw-Hill, 1949. Reprint, Liguori, Mo.: Triumph Books, 1996.

The Priest Is Not His Own. New York: McGraw-Hill, 1963. Reprint, San Francisco: Ignatius Press, 2004.

The Quotable Fulton Sheen: A Topical Compilation of the Wit, Wisdom, and Satire of Archbishop Fulton J. Sheen. New York: Doubleday, 1989.

These Are the Sacraments. New York: Hawthorn Books, 1962.

This Is the Holy Land. 1st ed. New York: Hawthorn Books, 1961.

This Is Rome. 1st ed. New York: Hawthorn Books, 1960.

Those Mysterious Priests. Garden City, N.Y.: Doubleday, 1974. Reprint, New York: St. Pauls, 2014.

Three to Get Married. New York: Appleton-Century-Crofts. 1951. Reprint, Princeton, N.J.: Scepter Publishers, 1996.

Treasure in Clay: The Autobiography of Fulton J. Sheen. Garden City, N.Y.: Doubleday, 1980. Reprint, San Francisco: Ignatius Press, 1993.

The World's First Love: Mary, Mother of God. New York: McGraw-Hill, 1952. This edition published with permission of the Society for the Propagation of the Faith. Reprint, San Francisco: Ignatius Press, 2011.